PADI® Divemaster Manual

PADI® Divemaster Manual

Editor in Chief Drew Richardson

Written by Alex Brylske

Edited by Mary Ellen Beveridge, Tonya Palazzi

Design and Production by Greg Beatty, Joe De La Torre, Jean Kester, Joy Lobell Zuehls

Photography by Frank Palazzi

Typography by Jeanne Jenkins, Don Osborne, Dail Schroeder

Illustrated by Nick Fain

Additional photos by Harry Averill, Al Hornsby, Mark M. Lawrence, Henrik Nimb, Drew Richardson, Dianne Weltlin, Bob Wohlers, Cayman Islands News Bureau

Consultants: Bruce Bassett, Ph.D., Dudley Crosson, Ph. D., Chris Wachholz — The Divers' Alert Network (DAN), Drew Richardson, Dr. Raymond E. Rogers, Capt. Steve Westervelt, Bob Wohlers

The PADI Headquarters Staff would like to express appreciation to all PADI Master Instructors, Course Directors and Dive Store Owners who offered their recommendations on Divemaster training. Without their cooperative efforts, this manual would not have been possible.

PADI®
Divemaster
Manual

© International PADI, Inc. 1985, 1990, 1991
All rights reserved. No part of this book may be reproduced in any form
without written permission of the publisher

Published by PADI, 1251 East Dyer Road #100, Santa Ana, CA 92705-5605 USA

Library of Congress Card Number 90-063863
ISBN 1-878663-07-0

Printed in the United States of America
10 9 8 7 6 5 4 3 2

PRODUCT NO. 70090 (Revised 8/91)

Contents

One

Course Orientation and the Role of the Divemaster

Section Objectives

☐ **Explain the prerequisites for becoming a Divemaster and contrast the nature of Divemaster training with other levels of diver training.**

☐ **Explain the four goals of the PADI Divemaster course and the general requirements for the three required training modules.**

☐ **Describe ten functions that a Divemaster may be expected to perform while acting in a supervisory capacity.**

☐ **List four benefits of PADI Divemaster Membership.**

Orientation

In most cases, what a diver has been trained to do is evident in the very title of the particular certification level. An Advanced Open Water Diver is one who has been oriented to advanced diving techniques; a Rescue Diver is one who is trained in diver-rescue techniques. Similarly, what a Specialty Diver is qualified to do is exemplified by the name of the certification itself — Wreck Diver, Deep Diver, Ice Diver and

1

Figure 1-1
First and foremost,
the Divemaster is one
who is responsible.

so on. However, this relationship is not exemplified in one particular certification level — the PADI Divemaster.

As we shall see, it is difficult to establish a precise definition for the term *PADI Divemaster* because the role is so diverse. There is, however, one common characteristic in virtually all definitions of *Divemaster* that is helpful in understanding just what is meant by the term. This characteristic is *responsibility.* No other single term so adequately defines what a Divemaster is. The Divemaster is responsible for people, responsible for planning, responsible for orienting, and at some time, responsible for nearly every aspect of safe diving.

This responsibility is a considerable one, and, therefore, the decision to become a qualified PADI Divemaster is not one that should be made hastily. The rewards of being a Divemaster, however, in terms of personal satisfaction and achievement, are unparalleled.

For those who decide that scuba diving can be more than a recreational endeavor and are interested in exploring the professional potential it may hold, acquiring the PADI Divemaster rating is an essential step in the process. The decision to pursue this goal is to be commended, and it is PADI's hope that this course will only be the beginning of a journey that will take the serious diver into an entirely different realm of diving — the realm of the professional.

Prerequisites

Figure 1-2
The PADI Divemaster rating
is the first step in your journey
to become a diving professional.

Traditionally, Divemaster courses have included a heavy emphasis on diver-rescue training. In the PADI training progression, however, rescue training is considered a distinct level of competence and a *prerequisite* to Divemaster training. Therefore, in order to qualify for PADI Divemaster Training, one must first be certified as a PADI Rescue Diver and have at least 20 logged dives. In addition, due to legal considerations, PADI Divemaster candidates must be eighteen years of age or older.

Other essential Divemaster prerequisites are not as easi-

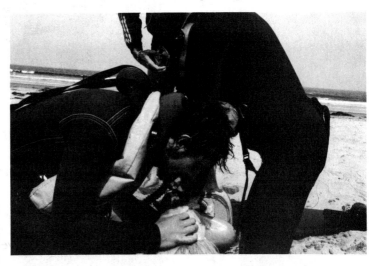

Figure 1-3
Developing competency in handling div-
ing emergencies is the primary reason
PADI Rescue Diver Training is a pre-
requisite to becoming a PADI Divemaster.

ly defined. Divemasters must possess emotional maturity in order to take on the responsibility for the safety of others. Likewise, an equally high degree of physical stamina and diving skill — much more so than that required for the average diver — is crucial in fulfilling the role of Divemaster.

Program Overview

To ensure high quality, the PADI Divemaster course was thoroughly tested and refined to make it one of the very finest programs of diver education in existence. The goals of the course are as follows:

1. To enable the candidate to organize, conduct and supervise diving activities, both land- and boat-based.

2. To enable the candidate to act effectively as an instructional assistant to a certified PADI Instructor.

3. To develop the candidate's theoretical diving knowledge to a level sufficient to become an Instructor.

4. To encourage and prepare the candidate for Instructor training.

To accomplish these objectives, PADI Divemaster Training is divided into three distinct phases or modules, each designed with specific performance objectives in mind.

Module One

Module One is designed to assess and, if necessary, provide

PADI DIVEMASTER COURSE

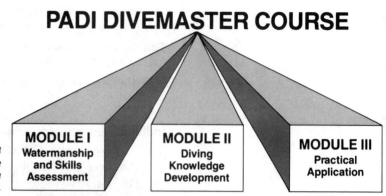

MODULE I	MODULE II	MODULE III
Watermanship and Skills Assessment	Diving Knowledge Development	Practical Application

Figure 1-4
The PADI Divemaster course
is designed to provide the utmost in
academic, skill and practical training.

remedial training in general watermanship and diving skills. Additionally, the candidate's diver-rescue ability will be assessed (this is why PADI Rescue Diver certification is a prerequisite), and he will be provided an opportunity to develop proficiency in dealing with stress-inducing problems. These latter two aspects of training are of vital importance when supervising student divers. The instructor will provide more detailed guidance during this phase of training.

Module Two

This training module is designed to increase knowledge of the theory and principles of diving. Using this manual and other PADI texts, the Divemaster candidate will study the topics of: dive planning; dive control and management; supervision of students in addition to diving physics; diving physiology; equipment; diving skills and environment; and the Recreational Dive Planner. The Instructor may elect to hold formal classroom sessions to present this information, or development may take place on a more individualized, self-paced basis. Candidates will complete a series of written examinations on these topics, and the Instructor will provide details.

Module Three

This training module involves training and experience in the supervisory aspect of being a Divemaster. This experience may be accomplished by two options. The first option involves taking part in specific classroom sessions and practical exercises designed to increase one's knowledge and awareness as a guide, supervisor and instructional assistant. The second option involves an internship during which the Divemaster candidate will serve as an instructional assistant to a qualified PADI Instructor. The objectives are to gain familiarity with the diver-training process, develop an awareness of typical student problems, and learn how to supervise and control divers in general. The internship requires the Divemaster candidate to take part in several pool and open-water training sessions in conjunction with other levels of PADI training. The Instructor will conduct candidate-performance evaluations during this training module using specific criteria and will maintain a record of performance. More on this aspect of training will be discussed in "Supervising Students in Training."

Figure 1-5
A qualified PADI Instructor can provide details on the practical phases of Divemaster training.

Scheduling

Because the nature of Divemaster training is so unique and because flexibility is needed, there are several scheduling options left to the discretion of the Instructor. A particular course schedule will be dependent upon considerations, such as available facilities, weather and the number of candidates in the class. Details will be provided by the Instructor.

Use of This Book

This manual was developed to provide detailed background information on the most vital aspects of being a Divemaster. Additionally, the manual was designed for use with PADI's *Adventures in Diving — Advanced Training for Open Water Divers,* the PADI *Rescue Diver Manual, The Encyclopedia of Recreational Diving* PADI's *Diving Knowledge Workbook,* and *The Recreational Diver's Guide to Decompression Theory, Dive Tables and Dive Computers*; the reader will frequently be referred to these texts as a knowledge refresher. It is also recommended that the Divemaster candidate obtain a copy of the PADI *Instructor Manual* to become familiar with PADI training standards and techniques.

This manual is divided into seven sections, each designed to present a different topic concerning the supervision of divers. The second and third sections address general concepts and procedures applicable to the supervison of *all* diving activities. The fourth section deals with the unique

Divemaster Manual Structure

OVERVIEW	**One** Course Orientation and the Role of the Instructor
GENERAL GUIDELINES	**Two** Dive Planning **Three** Dive Management and Control **Four** Supervising Students in Training
SPECIAL APPLICATIONS	**Five** Boat Diving Supervision and Control **Six** Deep Diving Supervision: Theory and Practice **Seven** Supervision of Specialized Diving Activities

Figure 1-6
The structure of this manual
is designed to gradually proceed from
the very general to the very specific.

concerns of handling student divers. The fifth, sixth and seventh sections cover procedures and vital background information on supervising various specialized diving activities. Some of the information contained in the latter sections may not be relevant to all Divemaster candidates, due to some candidates' specific local environments. Still, the candidate should become generally familiar with this information, because he may occasionally be responsible for supervising these types of activities.

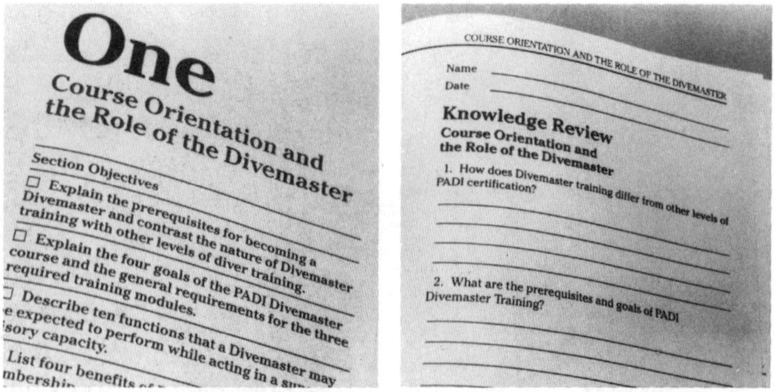

Figure 1-7
This manual was designed
for optimal learning effectiveness
by including devices, such as overt
objectives, review questions and ample
note-taking space in the margins.

A series of objectives is provided before each section. These objectives are useful in helping to focus attention on critical information while reading the material. Therefore, the objectives should be studied prior to reading each section. At the conclusion of each section there is a Knowledge Review. This exercise is designed to aid learning and retention of the material presented in the section. Upon completion, answers to the Knowledge Review may be compared to those in the answer key contained in the Appendix.

This manual will be of practical value even to those who are not involved in or have already completed PADI Divemaster Training. The topics discussed are important to anyone who may assume responsibility for supervising other divers.

The Role of the Divemaster

There is probably no other term in diving with a more diverse meaning than Divemaster. Traditionally, this term has been used to denote one who is "in charge" of a diving activity or a dive site. On closer examination, however, it is easy to see that a Divemaster may or may not be the individual in charge. Even more importantly, some of the functions that the Divemaster is expected to fulfill seem well beyond the realm of what may be considered a diving activity.

What are some of the roles a Divemaster *may be* called upon to fulfill? The list is long and extremely varied.

The Divemaster may act as a *guide*. It is very common for a Divemaster to act as an in-water tour guide who ensures that those in his charge have a safe, enjoyable diving experience. This is probably the most typical role.

The Divemaster may act as a *supervisor*. Instead of being responsible for a particular group of divers, he may be in charge of *all* divers in a group. This duty requires more training and experience than the role of a guide and often requires that

Figure 1-8
As a diving supervisor, the Divemaster must shift his primary emphasis from a concern for himself to a concern for others.

the Divemaster maintain an out-of-water vantage point so that he may oversee *all* aspects of the diving activity.

The Divemaster may perform as an *instructional assistant.* Although he is not qualified to teach independently, a primary role of the Divemaster is to act as an instructional assistant during diver-training courses. This role requires an extremely high degree of care, since those in the Divemaster's charge may not be fully qualified divers. As this may be the Divemaster's most important function, a major portion of PADI Divemaster Training will emphasize this vital role.

The Divemaster may act as a *medic.* If an accident occurs, first aid is essential. The individual who will be looked to for

Figure 1-9
One of the most important
functions of a PADI Divemaster
is his role as an instructional assis-
tant during diver-training activities.

such assistance is usually the Divemaster. Competency in first aid and emergency procedures is an unequivocal requirement of the effective Divemaster. To help fulfill this role, the Divemaster will draw upon the training received in

Figure 1-10
Because he is in charge,
the Divemaster's duties often involve
interpersonal skills and other matters
involving public relations.

the prerequisite PADI Rescue Diver course.

The Divemaster may act as an *oceanographer.* The typical motivation for many divers is to "see what's down there." Unfortunately, divers don't often know just what they are seeing. Divers will usually turn to the Divemaster as the source of information and expect a certain degree of expertise concerning the diving environment.

The Divemaster may function as a *technician.* Diving is an equipment-intensive activity, and equipment tends to need continual maintenance and repair. But, when maintenance and repair must be effected in the field, and more specifically *at the dive site,* the Divemaster is often called upon to perform these tasks. Obviously, technical skills in this area are invaluable assets to the Divemaster. Factory-authorized training and the PADI Equipment Specialist course are also suggested to improve one's capability in this area.

The Divemaster may serve as a *counselor.* As with any activity involving people, human-relations skills are crucial to success. Divers are often subjected to stress and anxiety, which must be dealt with in order to ensure safety. In the nondiving world, those who deal with these situations are called *counselors;* in the diving world, they are often called Divemasters.

The Divemaster may need to become a *public-relations expert.* The all-important aspect of return business is entirely dependent upon the diver (customer) having a safe, enjoyable experience. Whether self-employed or employed by someone else, the Divemaster is expected to be at the divers' disposal to ensure both diver safety *and* enjoyment. The Divemaster candidate should never make the mistake of assuming that the job of the Divemaster ends when divers are safely out of the water.

The Divemaster may function as a *seaman.* Many diving activities originate from boats. In fact, in many instances the Divemaster may be responsible for operating the vessel. Boat diving will, at the very least, require a high degree of familiarity with general boat operation and seamanship skills. This becomes particularly important when considering that divers themselves often have little boating experience or knowledge.

Finally, the Divemaster may act as a *trained buddy.* Although this role may sound unusual, consider the following: a Divemaster is specifically trained to deal with other divers — to supervise them, to assist them and to advise them. There is literally no better qualified diving buddy than a well-trained Divemaster.

Figure 1-11
The Divemaster is often called on to be a
seaman as well as a diving supervisor.

Such diversity may initially seem perplexing. In fact, the PADI Divemaster course can provide training in only the most vital of these functions. For many, however, it is just such diversity that makes the job of the Divemaster so interesting, exciting and rewarding.

Additionally, PADI hopes that the candidate's training will not end at the Divemaster level. As many of the training objectives in this course have been specifically designed to prepare candidates for Instructor training, Divemasters are encouraged to pursue even higher levels of professional training. Information on becoming a qualified PADI Open Water Scuba Instructor may be obtained from a local 5 Star Instructor Development Center or directly from PADI Headquarters.

COURSE DIRECTOR

MASTER INSTRUCTOR

IDC STAFF INSTRUCTOR

MASTER SCUBA DIVER TRAINER

SPECIALTY INSTRUCTOR

MEDIC FIRST AID INSTRUCTOR

OPEN WATER INSTRUCTOR

ASSISTANT INSTRUCTOR

DIVEMASTER

PADI Professional Continuing Education Progression

Figure 1-12

The PADI Divemaster

PADI Divemaster Training is the finest, most thorough in existence. In addition, PADI provides specific duties, responsibilities and benefits to its Divemasters.

PADI Membership

One of the most important benefits of successfully completing Divemaster training is full membership in the PADI association. PADI members are entitled to a subscription to *The Undersea Journal* (PADI's quarterly instructional publication), updates to PADI standards and programs, low-cost professional liability insurance and special prices on various product offers.

Insurance

PADI Divemaster members qualify to purchase PADI Professional Liability Insurance. This is the exact coverage provid-

Figure 1-13
The benefits of PADI Divemaster Membership are numerous.

ed to all insured PADI Instructors; but as Divemasters are not allowed to teach independently, the premium is less expensive. Insurance coverage is *highly* recommended, particularly for those who expect to engage in independent supervisory activities, such as organizing tours or working on dive-charter boats.

Summary

In the first portion of this section we addressed the unique nature of Divemaster training by stressing the concept of *responsibility.* We also discussed the prerequisites for Divemaster training in addition to the course goals and a brief training overview. We mentioned various scheduling considerations and how to use this text.

In the next portion of this section we detailed the varied roles that a Divemaster may assume in his normal course of duties. Although some are beyond the scope of this course, some of the duties a Divemaster may be expected to perform are: guide, supervisor, instructional assistant, medic, oceanographer, technician, counselor, public-relations expert, seaman and *trained buddy.* In the conclusion of this section we discussed the benefits of PADI Divemaster Membership.

Much of the PADI Divemaster course was designed with the assumption that the candidate will continue on to Instructor training. Significant portions of PADI Divemaster Training, such as watermanship/skill assessment and knowledge development, will prepare the candidate for this experience (in addition to being essential in carrying out the duties of a Divemaster). PADI is confident that the training received in this course will provide a firm base on which additional professional-level training can be built.

Figure 1-14
The PADI Divemaster — the
responsibility is considerable ... but
the rewards are worth it!

Notes:

Name _____

Date _____

Knowledge Review
Course Orientation and
the Role of the Divemaster

1. How does Divemaster training differ from other levels of PADI certification?

_____

_____

_____

_____

2. What are the prerequisites and goals of PADI Divemaster Training?

_____

_____

_____

_____

3. Explain the general requirements for each of the three training modules contained in the PADI Divemaster course.

_____

_____

_____

_____

4. List and describe ten functions that a Divemaster may be expected to perform.

_____

_____

_____

_____

_____

_____

_____

_____

_____

_____

5. List the four benefits of PADI Divemaster Membership.

_____

_____

_____

_____

Two

Dive Planning

Section Objectives

☐ **Demonstrate familiarity with a local open-water dive site by constructing a map of the underwater terrain and significant land features.**

☐ **Describe a procedure for diver assessment that will determine both experience and apprehension levels of divers.**

☐ **Explain how to evaluate the environmental conditions of any dive site in order to determine its acceptability for safe diving activities.**

☐ **Describe how the Divemaster may assist others in assessing the potential danger presented by marine life, and how the marine environment can best be protected.**

Introduction

The job of the Divemaster begins long before divers actually enter the water. In this section, we will examine dive *planning*. For the purposes of this manual, dive planning will be considered to be all preparatory activities necessary to the safe conduct of a dive occurring up to (although not including) the dive briefing. This section will also assume a typical recreational diving scenario that does *not* involve training activities.

Prior to reading this section you should already be familiar with general dive-planning procedures and in-depth background material regarding the marine environment. You can gain a more through the understanding of the marine environment by reviewing section Four: "The Aquatic Realm" of *The Encyclopedia of Recreational Diving* before proceeding with this section.

While planning a dive may be a relatively simple process for the individual diver, it is a far more complex process for the Divemaster. Supervisory personnel, such as the Divemaster, must be concerned not only with one diver but with *all* divers. And your list of responsibilities may entail more than strictly diving-related activities. Most often, the dive objective and the related logistical considerations will determine your role as Divemaster during the dive. When dealing with large groups who require distant travel, it may be your responsibility to arrange diver transport and diver accommodations. In other situations, you may be responsible for operating the dive boat. Regardless of the specific circumstances, you will soon realize that a Divemaster's job begins long before he arrives at the dive site.

Another vital aspect of dive planning is its instructional value to the divers involved. A proper and meticulously planned dive that results in a safe and enjoyable experience will best demonstrate the value of the phrase, "Always plan your dive." For the average diver, the common problems encountered in dive planning result more from not *knowing*

Figure 2-1
Because of his supervisory role, dive planning can be a complex process for the Divemaster.

Figure 2-2
An important job for the Divemaster is to teach others how to plan a dive properly.

how rather than not *wanting* to plan the dive. Watching an experienced, well-trained Divemaster is one of the best ways to learn the intricacies of dive planning, and no Divemaster should ever lose sight of this *instructive* aspect of how well — or how poorly — he does his job.

To become a competent dive planner, you must consider more than generalities. Your effectiveness as a Divemaster depends upon knowing *specifics.* Dive planning enables you to evaluate and make informed decisions concerning the conduct and control of the dive. Regardless of the dive objective, location or experience-level of those involved, proper dive planning involves two components: 1) *familiarization* and 2) *assessment.* Mastering these components will enable you to evaluate and make informed decisions regarding the conduct and control of a dive.

Familiarization

Familiarization is a process of collecting enough information about the divers and the dive site to make a valid assessment. Before you begin the assessment process, you must first be knowledgeable and familiar with what factors will affect your planning decisions.

Diver Familiarity

The Divemaster should be familiar with the divers in his charge. Ideally, he should have had prior experience with these individuals, which may have developed through prior relationships, such as having served as an assistant during their training course or through prior diving activities. It is unreasonable, however, to expect to be familiar with *all* those involved in the dive. In fact, some of the most difficult problems facing you as a Divemaster will result from your

Figure 2-3
It is beneficial for the Divemaster to quickly establish a rapport with those in his charge.

lack of familiarity with the divers. For this reason, the development of various assessment techniques is necessary and will be discussed shortly.

Dive Site Familiarity

It is extremely difficult for the Divemaster to adequately fulfill his responsibility for the supervision of other divers unless he is personally familiar with the dive site. Being

Figure 2-4
Being familiar with the dive site is important in maintaining adequate supervision.

thoroughly familiar with the dive site will enable you to: exercise better control of the diving activity; enable you to provide information to divers on where and when to dive; and, in the event of an emergency, will enable you to efficiently manage/search the scene. Familiarization will, therefore, require you to have prior experience at the particular dive site.

Familiarity with a *new* dive site is best accomplished by a survey of the area. However, without some means of organizing and recording the survey, your awareness will be limited to only that which can be committed to memory. Constructing an underwater map is, by far, the best way to overcome this inadequacy. For this reason, constructing such a map is a required part of PADI Divemaster Training.

Underwater Mapmaking

Reasonably accurate underwater maps are easy and fun to construct. To do so, you will need the following materials:

Figure 2-5
Mapmaking skills are useful in developing complete familiarity with a dive site.

1. Large underwater slate
2. Compass
3. PADI Divemaster Slate No. 5
4. Lines, weights and buoys
5. Graph paper

Recreating an accurate representation of the dive site should be the primary objective in constructing an under-

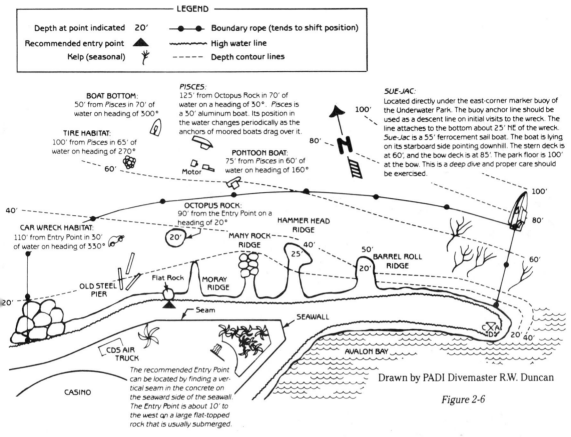

Drawn by PADI Divemaster R.W. Duncan

Figure 2-6

water map. Once completed, the map should include: 1) significant above- and below-water features indicated by appropriate symbols; 2) contours of the underwater terrain and bottom type/configurations; and 3) entry and exit locations (see Figure 2-6).

Before you begin working on the map, it is essential that you learn as much as you can about the dive site. You may do this by obtaining a detailed map or nautical chart that includes the area to be surveyed. Additionally, when you survey a completely unfamiliar dive site or areas within the site, it is best to make a *series* of orientation dives to better develop your general sense of awareness.

As you begin constructing the map, mark the location of any significant details with color-coded buoys so that their relative location can be accurately plotted once you are back on shore (be sure to record what feature each buoy is assigned to). Next, determine the position of other underwater features or objects via surface range bearings. Finally, with the PADI Divemaster Slate No. 5, plot the location of the various features relative to the selected surface bearings and other underwater features.

Figure 2-7
Learn as much about the dive site as possible before an underwater survey.

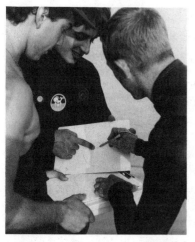

*Figure 2-8
Once back on shore, data collected
under water can easily be
transferred to graph paper.*

DIVER ASSESSMENT

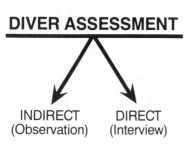

INDIRECT
(Observation)

DIRECT
(Interview)

Figure 2-9

After you return to shore, it will be simple to transfer the information from your slate to graph paper and to the desired scale. Add the location of the marker buoys to denote other features. Significant land features (including the objects used as ranges) can be added at the same time. Additional information on the construction of underwater maps is contained in the final chapter of the PADI publication, *Search and Recovery.*

Larger dive sites may be surveyed by using several divers and dividing the various areas or responsibilities among the group. Once you have practiced them, these procedures will greatly enhance your awareness of the underwater environment.

Assessment

The concept of *assessment* implies the need for the Divemaster to not only be aware of significant details, but to also make informed judgements and decisions with the information obtained. The assessment process applies to both the *divers* and the *diving environment.*

Diver Assessment

The assessment procedure used to make informed decisions about divers is both direct and indirect. *Indirect* assessment may be accomplished by subtle *observation,* while more *direct* assessment may be done by *interviews* or discussions with the divers.

The two areas you should be concerned with when observing divers are: 1) equipment and 2) behavior. Equipment considerations should include the *general condition* of the equipment (particularly of the scuba and buoyancy-

*Figure 2-10
Proper diver assessment requires
a high degree of astuteness and
good interpersonal skills.*

control systems) and *style* of the equipment (often of importance in determining the appropriateness for particular diving activities). An example of good equipment but wrong
style is a large, overweight diver about to make a deep dive
using a 50-cubic-foot/8-liter tank. While the *condition* of the
tank may be acceptable, the *style* (or in this case, capacity) of
the device may be inadequate, considering the individual
and the type of dive.

Another important consideration in observing divers is
the relative degree of rental versus owned equipment.
Although not an absolute rule, a diver using *primarily* rental
equipment may indicate either a general lack of familiarity
(after all, he does not own the equipment) or he may be
recently certified (most active divers own their equipment).
Generally, individuals with an overabundance of rental
equipment require your observation.

The behavioral considerations you should pay attention
to when observing divers are relative to:

1. The diver's apparent degree of familiarity with equipment and procedures

2. Signs of stress and the effect of peer pressure

3. Overdependence on a spouse or diving buddy

4. A diver taking an excessive amount of time to complete dive preparations (can indicate stress and/or a lack of
familiarity)

For a more in-depth examination of behavioral and
equipment-related problems, review "Section 1" and "Section 4," respectively, of the PADI *Rescue Diver Manual.*

Usually, you can obtain a more direct and accurate
assessment of a diver through informal, friendly discussion.

Figure 2-11
Much useful information can be gained
through a friendly, casual conversation.

Be sure, though, that you don't come across as though you are interrogating him. Instead, engage the diver in a casual conversation. In trying to make an informed assessment of the diver, try to determine the following:

1. The diver's certification level (not always entirely reliable, but helpful)

2. The *amount* and *type* of experience in addition to the date of the individual's last dive (review of the diver's log is the best way to accomplish this)

3. Any significant medical considerations, such as illness or recent injuries (medications taken, obvious physical impairments, extensive scar tissue, etc.)

4. A general impression of the individual's psychological condition (nervousness, apprehension, calm)

Another technique useful in direct assessment of divers is the use of an *emergency information card* (see Appendix). Particularly on formally organized dives, e.g. on a charterboat dive or diving vacations, useful information may be easily and systematically determined through the use of these cards or similar devices.

With training and experience, the Divemaster can assess a diver's ability subtly, thoroughly and without inconvenience. Probably no other skill is more important to the development of truly competent supervisory personnel than the ability to assess individual divers based on observation and discussion.

Environmental Assessment

An essential duty of the Divemaster is the evaluation of the environmental conditions (both present and anticipated) at the intended dive site. You should allow diving activities to

Figure 2-12
Proper evaluation of environmental conditions is a vital part of planning a safe dive.

take place *only* if conditions are acceptable. It must be understood, however, that the term *acceptable* is relative. For example, what is acceptable for a group of highly experienced divers in a familiar area may be totally unacceptable for inexperienced divers who are unfamiliar with the site. An additional complicating factor is that rarely is an informal group of divers homogeneously grouped according to experience and ability. All of these considerations make your final decision a difficult one in all but the most ideal conditions. Yet, in the interest of safety, such *go/no go* decisions must be made.

Even though you have the final responsibility for decision making, teaching others how to evaluate conditions also has great value. Remember, not all diving activities take place with a competently trained Divemaster in charge; therefore, one of your secondary objectives should always be to provide divers with the guidelines on how they may evaluate environmental conditions on an unsupervised dive.

Weather

Few other recreational activities are as controlled by weather conditions as diving is. The effects of weather not only determine the atmospheric conditions for the dive, but also greatly affect the surface and subsurface conditions of the water. Therefore, it is vital that you have a general understanding of how to determine and interpret weather conditions.

You can easily obtain weather forecasts before arriving at the dive site from newspapers, television or radio. Within the United States, more in-depth marine-oriented reports are provided by the National Weather Service through the National Oceanic and Atmospheric Administration (NOAA). Similar services are provided in many other countries. These broadcasts may be heard on VHF-FM radio receivers. The channels broadcasting these reports are 162.400 MHz, 162.475 MHz, or 16.550 MHz, depending upon the local area. Often these channels are marked on the radio receiver as *weather* or *WX*. VHF receivers may vary from the two-way marine radios common on most dive boats, to inexpensive radios specially designed to broadcast only weather information. In addition to radio broadcasts, many areas make prerecorded weather reports available over the telephone. If a sophisticated weather-forecasting service is not available to you, a good source for weather information may be a local airport or marine authority. You must be able to secure accu-

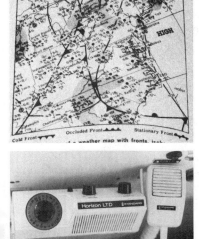

Figure 2-13
Sources of marine-weather information are readily available once you know where to look.

Figure 2-14
Learning how to interpret weather charts is a useful skill for the Divemaster.

rate information concerning weather conditions that could affect diving activities — regardless of circumstance.

Generally, weather patterns are caused by the interaction of warm equatorial air masses and cold polar air masses, which are both under the influence of the earth's rotation. At sea level, the standard air pressure is 1013.2 millibars, or 29.92 inches of mercury. Variations in this standard pressure occur at the surface because cold air is more dense and sinks, while warm air is less dense and rises. This interaction causes high- and low-pressure areas, which are responsible for the variation of weather.

As air pressure rises, it is able to hold vast amounts of invisible moisture. As air pressure falls, the air cools and moisture condenses into clouds, rain, fog and so on. This situation may be reversed as the air pressure begins to rise. Thus, high-pressure centers are associated with settled weather, and low-pressure centers are associated with unsettled weather.

The factor of weather that you in your role as Divemaster want particularly to be concerned with is the formation of wind. Especially important is your understanding that coastal winds often differ from those generally forecast. This can be a crucial consideration if planning a dive in a coastal area and the forecast on which decision making is based is not marine-oriented. Typically, you can expect calm wind conditions in the early morning. However, as the sun heats

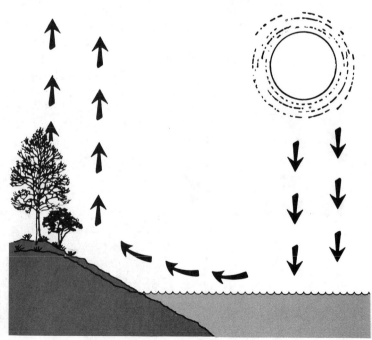

Figure 2-15
Warm air rising over the land is replaced by the cooler air sinking over the sea, which results in a sea breeze.

land masses far faster than water, the land quickly warms and forms an upward convection current. This current pulls the cooler air in from the sea and creates a sea breeze that tends to intensify until late afternoon. As the land cools, this breeze will gradually decrease and usually dissipates at night.

This phenomenon holds important implications for dive-planning purposes. One can usually expect dives planned for early morning hours or later in the evening to yield calmer wind conditions than during midday. This is not an absolute rule, however. Weather patterns can be far more intricate and can be affected by many other factors. What has just been described is a typical summertime weather pattern for coastal areas.

In addition to its effect on the environment, weather has equally significant effects upon the divers themselves. Adverse environmental conditions can have serious and dangerous consequences by requiring the expenditure of substantial energy reserves as in swimming against a current or in high surf. Weather is also responsible to a great extent for the single biggest environmental factor affecting all divers — cold. Diving should never be attempted without first considering weather conditions and its related effects upon the individual and the environment.

Figure 2-16
Proper planning can help avoid diving in adverse environmental conditions.

Tide and Currents

The currents that affect divers are usually *localized* and caused by *tidal exchange.* Therefore, the Divemaster should be able to read a tide chart to predict tide levels. As a general rule, diving at high tide yields the best visibility. Additionally, graphic tide charts (such as those depicted in Figure 2-17)

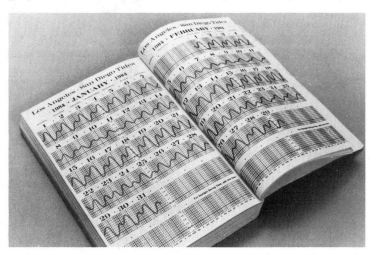

Figure 2-17
Knowing how to read a tide chart is an important skill for the Divemaster.

provide a comparative basis for determining the relative strength of current. Be sure to note any days when there is a great variation between high and low tide. Logically, it is easy to understand that on such days, when vast amounts of water must be exchanged between high and low tide, local currents will tend to be stronger than on days with minimal tidal exchange.

Ideally, if tidal current could have a significant effect, dives should be planned to take place during *slack tide*. This is the point at which tidal currents cease in preparation for the change in the opposite direction (high to low or vice versa). Determining the precise time of slack tide for a particular locale can be difficult, as it can be subject to many local factors. But, when it becomes necessary to dive at slack tide, you may obtain precise information from the *Tidal Current Charts* published by the National Ocean Survey. These tables provide virtual worldwide coverage. The publication even contains instructions on how to use it. If detailed charts are not available, consult local fishermen and boat operators — they may yield useful information.

One additional word of caution regarding currents. Never assume that a current will always flow in one and only one direction. This is particularly true with *longshore* currents, which may interact with major oceanic currents. For

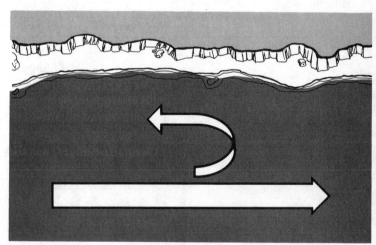

Figure 2-18
Counter currents or eddies can often develop off of a major longshore current.

example, because the Gulf Stream flows from south to north along the U.S. east coast, it may appear logical to assume that all longshore currents on the eastern U.S. coast flow at all times in a northerly direction. Practical experience shows that this is not true. This is because major oceanic currents are not the only cause of localized currents; in fact, it is not uncommon for eddies to develop in a direction *opposite* to the major current. Local physical features can also greatly affect the direction and behavior of current. It takes extensive experience with a specific dive site to gain a full understanding of the behavior of local currents.

To be certain that you have the best vantage point, it is best to determine the presence and direction of a current from high ground. You should watch for flotsam in the water or boats at anchor to determine the direction and relative strength of the current. Make sure the current is moving the flotsam, and not the wind. Occasionally, strong wind can push floating objects *against* a mild current. With this in mind, it is obvious that the important information to the diver is the current, not the wind. Likewise, the direction of

Figure 2-19
In open ocean, currents along the bottom can, at times, run counter to surface currents, and the Divemaster must be prepared for this.

subsurface currents is occasionally inconsistent with the direction of the surface current and can have significant impact on dive planning. This phenomenon occurs particularly in open, deep water — such as the type that would be encountered while boat diving.

When supervising divers in the presence of currents, there are specific considerations you should always keep in mind. First, a diver can only swim against the slightest current (usually less than two knots) and even then only for a short distance. See to it that the divers use the current as an

27

Figure 2-20
It is crucial that divers be
instructed how to react in the event
they are carried away by current.

aid — particularly at the end of the dive when the diver is most tired. This consideration is especially important when selecting entry and exit points from shore. Second, never assume that because the current is flowing in one direction that it cannot, or will not, change direction. The observant Divemaster must pay constant attention to determine any changes in the current that could affect divers who are already in the water.

If a diver should become caught in a strong current, you should instruct him *not* to fight it. Instead, if the diver is unable to proceed against the current, have him establish positive buoyancy and rest and drift *with* the current. You should then dispatch assistance from the shore or boat to retrieve the diver.

Visibility Factors

Many divers consider visibility to be the single most important factor in selecting a dive site. Visibility is also likely to be

Figure 2-21
Being prepared to deal with visibility
that is poorer than expected is an
important guideline to follow.

a major factor in determining the level of enjoyment the diver receives from the underwater experience. With such importance ascribed to underwater visibility, it would be justified to consider what factors affect visibility and how the Divemaster can use this information in dive-site selection and planning.

Factors affecting visibility are:

1. Weather
2. Seasonal variation
3. Bottom composition
4. Wave action or surge
5. Time of day
6. Currents
7. Location

In actuality, each of these factors affect the relative degree/source of suspended particulate in the water and the amount of light that can penetrate the water.

Weather, which is also related to *seasonal variation*, has several effects on visibility. For example, rain can significantly increase the amount of particulate in the water both directly and by runoff flowing into the water from shore. Additionally, temperature extremes during summer months can produce explosive amounts of plankton, due to the nutrient-

Figure 2-22
Weather and seasonal variation can have positive and negative effects upon visibility.

rich water conditions. This phenomenon is sometimes referred to as a *plankton bloom* — a commonly known form of which is red tide. Therefore, all other factors aside, visibility in most areas tends to be better in the winter due to the decreased level of plankton. Also, changes in the thermal stratification of water (particularly in fresh water) brought about by seasonal changes in air temperature can greatly

Figure 2-23
When possible, plan diving activities in areas with hard or course bottom characteristics (bottom), and not in areas prone to silting (top).

Figure 2-24
The amount of light that can penetrate the water is determined by absorption and diffusion.

affect visibility.

The effects of *bottom composition, wave action* and *surge* upon visibility are more obvious. Severe "chop" or wave action can drastically decrease the amount of light penetrating the water. Bottom composition is important for other reasons. Essentially, the finer the substance that comprises the bottom, the easier it is for that substance to become suspended in the water. The easier the substance can become suspended, the more easily visibility can be decreased by water motion (as in the action of waves or surge). Mud, silt and fine-sand bottoms, because of their delicate and suspendible nature, are much more prone to cause decreased visibility conditions. Conversely, gravel, hard-packed clay, course sand, coral or rock are not prone to suspension and are, therefore, much less affected by water motion. For optimal visibility, select dive sites with consolidated bottom materials whenever possible.

Often the *time of day* at which a dive is to be made is not considered significant. This is a mistake that can seriously impede underwater visibility. When light strikes the surface of the water at an angle of less that 48°, most of it will be

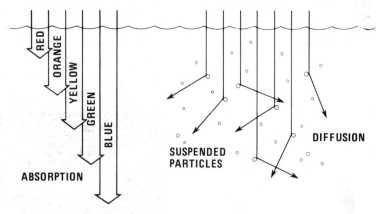

deflected. At higher angles, much more light can penetrate. Because of this fact, the highest levels of light penetration (and, therefore, the greatest amount of visibility) will occur between 10 a.m. and 2 p.m. Though other factors may prevent it (such as changing weather conditions), try to plan diving activities during times of optimal light penetration.

Major oceanic *currents* and the physical *location* of a dive site can have dramatic effects both upon underwater visibility and the entire ecological environment. The Gulf Stream is an excellent example of this phenomenon. Many divers are not aware of the tropical nature of the underwater environment at certain times of the year as far north as

North Carolina on the U.S. east coast. Under ideal summertime conditions, the warm and clear waters of the Gulf Stream pass offshore from this area, bringing conditions and marine life one may expect only much farther south. This also explains why an island as far north as Bermuda enjoys a tropical marine environment. Conversely, though one may expect an equally tropical environment in the warm climate of Southern California, this area is actually very temperate with surface water temperatures ranging from 55-70°F/12.7-21°C. All of these situations are examples of the effects of major oceanic currents, and are reflected in other areas of the world.

Another effect of ocean currents on visibility is relative to the amount of nutrients (and, therefore, suspended particulate) that are held in the water. Warm tropical water usually remains relatively low in nutrients and tends to be very clear, except during seasonal plankton blooms. Colder ocean currents, conversely, give rise to continually high concentrations of nutrients and provide lesser-quality visibility.

Figure 2-25
The Gulf Stream is a classic example how major oceanic currents affect the environment.

Marine Life

The impact that marine life has upon divers is very intriguing because it is both positive and negative. Although unjustified, few things are more frightening to divers than their perceptions of the dangers of marine life. Yet, the main motivation for most divers is the experience of witnessing a whole new environment that contains this marine life. This

Figure 2-26
The attitude that divers have toward marine life and the underwater environment can be greatly influenced by the Divemaster.

apparent dilemma is important to you in your role as Divemaster; it is your job to strike a balance between the rational and irrational views of divers. You must be able to put the relative potential danger of marine life into the proper perspective without conveying that the entire marine environment is harmless. Your goal must be to help divers develop healthy, reasonable respect for the marine environment.

To do his job effectively, the Divemaster must possess a good knowledge of marine life. It is very beneficial for you to research and understand the marine ecosystem you are likely to encounter. You can accomplish this through taking a PADI Research Diver course or a PADI Distinctive Specialty

Figure 2-27
Divers can learn more about the marine environment through PADI Distinctive Specialty training and other sources.

like Marine Awareness. Marine-science courses are also available at local colleges or universities. Remember, in most diving situations, divers will look to you for answers.

A final consideration involves the Divemaster's role in seeing that marine life is protected. After all, divers have a very self-serving reason to see that the world's oceans and their inhabitants continue to thrive. Diving professionals, in particular, should appreciate the importance of this attitude. Disregard for ecology harms the planet and inhibits the livelihood of those who work in the outdoor environment. As an ecologically responsible Divemaster, you may want to observe the following guidelines:

1. Encourage divers to take only what game they can eat, *not* anything that isn't edible.

2. Require, where appropriate, that divers have the necessary licenses and use only sportsman-like, legal equipment to take game. Be certain to apprise divers of local game regulations *before* the dive. (In fact, some areas do not allow divers to take anything from the water at all.)

3. Discourage divers from touching, standing on, sitting on or in any way molesting hard coral. (Even slight disruption of the exterior layer of mucus can be fatal to the entire organism.)

4. Discourage the practice of feeding sea urchins and other marine life to fish. (Everything has its purpose in the ecosystem.)

5. Discourage divers from dislodging large rocks or other underwater habitat. (If they do so, be sure to replace the rocks in their original position.)

Figure 2-28
Being aware and respectful of ecology is one of the most critical attitudes the Divemaster can help foster in divers.

What is Project A.W.A.R.E.?

As the world's largest diver educational organization PADI will train nearly ten million new divers by the year 2000. As a result, we recognize that we have a responsibility to preserve the aquatic environment. Project A.W.A.R.E. (Aquatic World Awareness, Responsibility and Education) is PADI's 10-year plan to accomplish this.

Education

Education is PADI's field of expertise, and it is the most important aspect of Project A.W.A.R.E. Through PADI publications new training materials, advertising, publicity and presence at trade and consumer dive shows, we will stress the divers' role in preserving the environment. We hope that Project A.W.A.R.E. will be a rallying point for our more than 28,000 members and 1,400 Dive Centers worldwide, who will instill in their students and customers good environmental sense along with safe diving practices. We want PADI divers to be welcome guests wherever they venture.

Communication

PADI's network of diving and marine professionals is international and extensive. We've created an environmental Advisory Committee comprised of leaders in the marine sciences and environmentalism to help guide our efforts. PADI is also actively encouraging other environmental organizations to use our network and communications to reach divers and diving professionals worldwide. PADI can provide a link to millions of divers, who by their very nature are concerned about the environment. We will survey our members on an ongoing basis to explore the issues that are most significant to them and act accordingly on their behalf — whether it be through education, legislative efforts or taking a corporate stance.

Action

PADI continually monitors legislation regarding diver safety, divers' rights and its members' interests, and tries to respond quickly, when needed, with effective lobbying at all levels of government. PADI will also serve this "watch-dog" role on environmental legislation, particularly those issues that directly affect divers. At the grassroots level, PADI will inform its members of important legislation and activities regarding aquatic resources so that they may take action as they see fit. In terms of "hands-on" participation, PADI is working to organize its global membership to participate in an annual worldwide shoreline cleanup. Other such activities will develop as the program matures.

Commitment

January 1990, PADI Headquarters switched to recycled and biodegradable products in nearly all its operations. This includes using shredded paper instead of bubble wrap in shipping, printing as many of our brochures, flyers and stationary as possible on recycled paper, and even banishing plastic cups from our employees' lunchrooms. We encourage other recreational diving businesses to follow this example, and will be happy to supply information, upon request, on the sources of such materials to interested companies.

For the Rest of This Century

It's fitting that Project A.W.A.R.E. occupy the last decade of the twentieth century so that the twenty-first century might mark a new beginning. Recent popular interest in environmental issues has PADI optimistic that divers can make a difference. PADI is not trying to clean up the world. We're not big enough for that. But we are dropping pebbles into the water and letting the ripples spread. With Awareness, Responsibility and Education, hopefully this can add up to a tidal wave of action.

Dive Planning in Remote Areas

It is becoming increasingly popular for divers to venture into highly remote areas of the world to pursue their interests. This presents unique problems for the Divemaster who is attempting to plan such activities. In general, the guideline to planning diving activities in highly remote locations is to

Figure 2-29
Diving in highly remote locations
can present unusual obstacles
to dive planning.

assume that virtually no support services, or even information about these services, may be available.

The first problem the Divemaster must deal with is
logistics. Often, you will be responsible for making extensive
and highly unusual travel arrangements. You should assume
that any form of transportation will be unreliable and may be
inadequate. Therefore, you should always have a contingency plan for unforseen travel problems, if possible. Likewise, it
may also be necessary for food to be provided, transported
and distributed (this is an especially important consideration
for totally self-sustained groups). Also, do not overlook the
availability of air. Some locations may even require you to
make arrangements to bring a compressor! Finally, you should
ensure that all divers in the party have the appropriate travel
visas, passport endorsements and appropriate vaccinations.

In addition to logistical considerations, you should also
give attention to emergency procedures. Of particular importance is how, in the event of an emergency, a victim will be
evacuated to an appropriate facility. Transport of a sick or injured diver will typically require several hours of travel time,
and may necessitate sea-, land- and aircraft. To further complicate the matter, customs regulations might also affect
evacuation plans if international travel is required. (For international travel, even *emergency* flights are often required to
wait 24 hours for approval of the flight plan by the host
country.)

Under such unusual circumstances it is highly recommended that either the Divemaster or some other responsible person have advanced medical training. Divemasters
planning activities in remote locations would do well to
become paramedically trained, and have medical support
equipment with them which far exceeds the contents of a
typical first aid kit. In fact, the best solution to coordinating

emergency medical procedures is to contact a physician in the area to be visited for advice. Obviously, under such unusual and primitive conditions, the Divemaster should require divers to exercise considerable care and a conservative approach to all diving procedures, particularly those relating to decompression sickness. Generally, being "prepared for the worst" takes on a whole new meaning in many of the more exotic, yet remote, diving locations.

Summary

In this section we discussed various aspects of dive planning from the standpoint of those responsible for diver supervision. Dive planning was defined as those activities occurring prior to the dive briefing that are necessary to the safe conduct of a dive. More specifically, supervisory planning has two components — *familiarization* and *assessment*. These components relate to both divers and the diving environment.

We discussed several important concepts and procedures regarding the topic of familiarity. Generally, *familiarity* requires experience with individual divers and the dive site. Gaining experience of the dive site is facilitated by constructing an underwater map and conducting a survey.

We addressed the indirect means (such as observation) *and* the direct means (such as discussion) of *diver assessment*. Decisions concerning diver assessment are most often based upon input gathered from the individual's equipment, appearance, psychological condition and diving experience.

We saw that *environmental assessment* requires a very wide range of knowledge concerning topics, such as weather, tides and currents, and factors affecting visibility. Finally, this section concluded with a discussion of the Divemaster's role helping others to appreciate and protect the marine environment, and considerations when planning diving activities in highly remote locations.

The overall goal of this section was to present the criteria and considerations required for planning a dive for others. It is important to note that often the result of this evaluative process is the decision that a dive would *not* be in the best interest of safety. These *go/no-go* decisions are often difficult and certainly are not popular. The courage to enforce these decisions, however, can provide an important lesson for the divers involved. The instructive nature of a properly planned dive should teach not only what to consider *before* diving, but what considerations determine when a dive should *not* be made at all.

Figure 2-30
Part of the Divemaster's responsibility is deciding when in the interest of safety diving is not advised.

Notes:

Name _____

Date _____

Knowledge Review

Dive Planning

1. What are the two essential components of dive planning for the Divemaster?

_____

_____

_____

_____

2. Why is it necessary for the Divemaster to have a high degree of familiarity with both the divers in his charge and the dive site in general? How may such familiarity be accomplished?

_____

_____

_____

_____

3. By what *indirect* means can the Divemaster make an assessment of those divers in his charge? What specifically should be determined in making such an assessment?

_____

_____

_____

_____

4. By what *direct* means can the Divemaster make an assessment of those divers in his charge? What specifically should be determined in making such an assessment?

_____

_____

_____

_____

5. What factors make it difficult at times for the Divemaster to determine the "acceptability" of environmental conditions for diving?

_____

_____

_____

_____

6. By what means can the Divemaster obtain information of weather conditions?

_____

_____

_____

7. Relative to weather conditions, why is it usually more advisable to plan diving activities in coastal areas for early-morning hours?

_____

_____

_____

_____

8. What types of currents usually affect the diver? How may proper dive planning decrease the effect of currents?

_____

_____

_____

_____

9. Explain what procedure should be advised for a diver caught in a strong current.

_____

_____

_____

_____

10. List seven factors that can affect underwater visibility and describe significant characteristics about each.

_____

_____

_____

_____

11. What dilemma does the presence of marine life create for the diver? How can the Divemaster help overcome this problem?

_____

_____

_____

_____

12. List five guidelines the Divemaster can follow to help protect the marine environment of a dive site.

_____

_____

_____

_____

Three

Dive Management and Control

Section Objectives

☐ Define the term *control* and its requirements as it refers to diving activities.

☐ List and explain the functions of the various equipment items required by the Divemaster for the supervision and control of large-scale diving activities.

☐ List the procedures and information to be contained in a dive briefing and pre-dive safety check.

☐ Demonstrate an accounting procedure using the PADI Dive Roster that enables supervisory personnel to determine all necessary information required for effective dive control.

☐ Demonstrate the procedure for both the in-water and out-of-water control and supervision of divers.

☐ Demonstrate how to conduct a PADI Environmental Orientation dive consistent with PADI Standards.*

*Refers to the "Standards and Procedures" section of the Instructor Manual.

Introduction

This section will discuss what is probably the most important function of the Divemaster — the *management* and *control* of divers. As in Dive Planning, this section will assume a typical diving scenario that does *not* involve training activities. Most of what will be covered, however, is applicable to training *and* non-training situations. Additionally, this section will assume a land-based diving activity, as boat diving will be covered separately in a later section.

To fully understand the concept of dive management and control, one must first define the terms. In general, *manage* is defined as "to have charge of," and *control* is defined as "to exercise a restraining or directing influence

Figure 3-1
The management and control of divers is usually the Divemaster's most important function.

over." Both of these terms describe very accurately the primary role of the Divemaster.

While the term *management* may be used for the purposes of this section in its general sense, the term *control* requires a definition more specific to diving. Therefore, in the context of those responsible for the supervision of divers, control will be assumed to mean "the ability to *prevent* or *immediately respond* to a problem in order to avoid discom-

Figure 3-2
To control divers, the Divemaster
must not only be able to recognize
problems, but prevent them as well.

fort, injury or panic." The remainder of this section will detail how such control may be accomplished by the Divemaster.

Elements of Control

Four conditions are essential in excercising control during open-water diving activities. These include:

1. Preparation   3. Positioning
2. Communication   4. Recognition

Adequate *preparation* begins with the understanding and use of the guidelines discussed in the previous section on

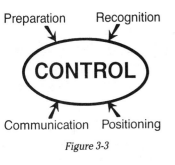

Figure 3-3

Figure 3-4
Many problems may be
prevented through recognition
of the factors that cause them.

Dive Planning. Additionally, preparation requires that the proper equipment and trained supervisory personnel are available.

Communication encompasses several aspects. Assuming that appropriate, sufficient communications equipment is on hand, one must also know the proper procedures for effective communication. The most crucial ingredient of communication for the Divemaster is the dive briefing. As the dive briefing is so vital to the safe and efficient organization of a dive, it will be extensively detailed in a later segment.

Proper *positioning* relates to how the Divemaster physically situates himself in order to be most effective. The Divemaster must determine this positioning with consideration to where problems are most likely to occur and to the number of supervisory personnel available at the dive site. In most noninstructional situations, the number of supervisory personnel is usually very limited, so this aspect of control requires careful thought.

Finally there is the element of *recognition.* The most useful definition of recognition for the Divemaster is the ability to *anticipate, identify* and *correct* mistakes or behaviors that indicate potential problems. Notice that this definition stresses the aspect of *prevention.* It is often said that "a good lifeguard is one who doesn't have to make rescues"; the same applies to a good Divemaster. Anyone can recognize a problem once it occurs. The professional, however, must be able to recognize situations that may lead to problems *before* they occur.

The concept of control can be compared to the stability of a chair. A chair with four legs is very stable. With only three legs, the chair's stability is severely decreased. With only one or two, stability is virtually impossible to maintain. Likewise, control of a dive can only be fully maintained if all four elements — preparation, communication, positioning and recognition — are present.

Equipment

There are various pieces of equipment that are either essential or convenient to dive control. Convenience items,

Figure 3-5
Some equipment items are essential to maintaining adequate control and supervision of a dive.

Figure 3-6
The Divemaster should consider some equipment items essential to maintaining adequate control and supervision of a dive.

however, should *not* be viewed as nonessentials, because a Divemaster should not only ensure the safety of a dive, but should ensure diver enjoyment, as well. Also assumed in this discussion is that both the Divemaster and his charges have and are using adequate personal diving equipment. Some of these items are more appropriate for larger groups, while others are useful regardless of group size. Reviewing the PADI *Rescue Diver Manual,* "Section 6" Equipment Considerations may also be helpful in determining what personal diving equipment is adequate. The following is a list of both essential and convenient equipment items.

1. Clipboard and dive roster
2. First-aid kit
3. Oxygen
4. Flotation/rescue device
5. Signaling/communication devices
6. "Extra" dive gear, maintenance and convenience items

Figure 3-7
Some equipment is designed
to prevent emergencies ...

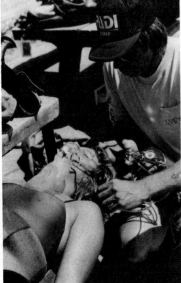

Figure 3-8
... others are designed to respond to them.

The *clipboard* and *dive roster* are essential items for maintaining an adequate accounting procedure and other vital diver information. (Maintaining an adequate accounting procedure and other vital diver information will be discussed in greater depth later.) Obviously, the clipboard should be suited to the marine environment and should be protected from water damage. The PADI Diver Roster is especially ideal for accounting and informational purposes.

First aid and *oxygen equipment* are among the most crucial items to have on hand at the dive site. Thoroughly reviewing "Section 2" of the PADI *Rescue Diver Manual* will help you determine the specifics of and uses for this equipment.

Flotation and rescue devices are vitally important in planning dive-control activities, though they are often overlooked. Though some may argue that any BCD should be adequate for flotation and rescue purposes, remember

Figure 3-9
A rescue board is an extremely useful device for both transport and support.

that a Divemaster strives for more than "adequacy." The Divemaster should consider using a rescue surfboard, which is extremely efficient for transporting supervisory personnel across the surface. Rescue surfboards also provide excellent surface stations at the scene of a problem and can be very useful in maintaining proper positioning by providing a higher vantage point in the water. Though somewhat less effective, inflatable mats may also be used for this purpose.

Signaling and communication devices vary according to both the size of the group and the nature of the dive. Surface communication with larger groups or across substantial distances can be greatly facilitated by the use of a bullhorn or PA system. Air horns make particularly good surface signaling devices. With larger groups using numerous supervisory personnel, walkie-talkies are useful — especially if they are equipped with multiple crystals, one of which is an emergency frequency. Other devices specific to certain specialized diving will be covered in later sections. Finally, a good pair of binoculars (waterproof, ideally) is essential to surface supervisory personnel.

Figure 3-10
When supervising large groups, it is helpful to have an efficient means of surface communication.

A wide range of items can be included in a discussion of "extra" dive gear, maintenance and convenience equipment. Inevitably, due to poor maintenance or forgetfulness, divers will occasionally need spare equipment. The Divemaster should always have at least one complete set of "spare" gear on hand. Because both large and small equipment items are often necessary to complete the set, the equipment list can become quite extensive. The term *"save-a-dive" kit* was appropriately coined to describe a suggested collection of "spare" diving equipment. Such "save-a-dive" accessories could include:

1. An assortment of tools
2. Mask and fin straps
3. O-rings and high-pressure plugs
4. Hose retainers (Tywraps)
5. Quick-release buckles
6. Silicone lubricant   *O-Ring pick*
7. Electrical tape
8. Neoprene glue
9. CO_2 cartridge
10. 50 feet of ⅛-inch nylon line
11. Appropriate decongestant tablets
12. Antacid tablets
13. Seasickness medication (a nontransdermal variety)
14. Suntan lotion with PABA

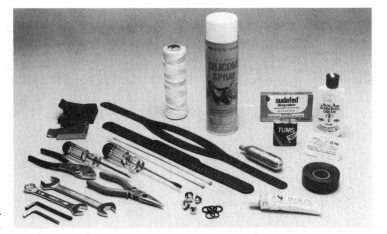

Figure 3-11
The "save-a-dive" kit — no Dive-
master should be without one.

The Dive Briefing

Because communication is an essential element of dive control, the *dive briefing* is the first and most important component of this communication requirement. Being concise during the dive briefing is extremely important, because the briefing is often the only opportunity a Divemaster has to speak formally and directly to everyone involved in the dive. A proper dive briefing will include both an *area briefing* and a *pre-dive safety check*.

Figure 3-12
The dive briefing often provides the only opportunity the Divemaster will have to talk to every diver; what he says must therefore be thorough yet concise.

Area Orientation

Each dive briefing should begin with an orientation to the available facilities. This discussion may include the location of restrooms, showers, food concessions, telephones and any other facilities that may be useful, convenient or essential to the divers. You should also explain any areas that are off-

Figure 3-13
The area orientation should include important, useful information, such as the depth range and general characteristics of the site.

limits to divers (such as private property or restricted areas).

The next point you should discuss in the briefing is the dive site itself. Begin by explaining the *general characteristics* of the site, including the bottom type and topography. Discussing the *depth range* of the site is also essential. The term *range* is used because a dive is rarely conducted at a single consistent depth. Divers must therefore know what depth range to plan for. The briefing should not be limited to safety-related information. Be sure to explain any special, interesting facets about the site or the particular environment the divers are about to experience.

Entry and exit considerations should be discussed next. Suggest not only when but *how* to enter and exit — particularly if the entry/exit is unique or particularly difficult. Proper positioning and assistance from supervisory personnel is especially helpful during this phase of the dive.

Figure 3-14
Entry considerations are often the most-variable factor in the briefing and should be addressed with special care.

In some situations, the Divemaster will have to make *buddy-team assignments*. This is less probable in noninstructional situations, but may still be necessary if some divers are strangers to the group and have no buddies. You should exercise care in this instance and use the assessment procedures described in Dive Planning. Avoid, particularly, pairing two inexperienced divers together.

Even in situations when there is no need to assign buddies (such as friends diving together), you should review basic buddy-diving procedures. Be certain to stress that bud-

Figure 3-15
Buddy-diving procedures should be a part of every dive briefing.

dies should remain at a distance *no greater than that from which they can provide assistance to each other.* Secondly, if buddies do become separated, after a *brief* (less than a minute) search they should ascend to the surface to regroup.

You may also wish to review some *general safety rules* to alleviate later confusion. All Divemasters must be familiar with the PADI Safe Diving Practices (provided in the Appendix) and must use this information as a guide when discussing safety procedures. It is also important to review significant hand signals. Reviewing hand signals is especially important in resort areas that attract divers from highly diverse training backgrounds.

Communication and *emergency procedures* are two other vital portions of the dive briefing. One useful communication/emergency procedure that you may suggest is to require that divers give you the "OK" signal every time they surface. (That way, any diver not giving the "OK" signal upon surfacing should be perceived as being in trouble.) You

Figure 3-16
No briefing should be considered
complete without a review of basic
communication, such as hand signals.

should also inform divers of what they should do and how they will be recalled from the water if a problem occurs. Do *not,* however, dwell on emergency procedures that are important only for supervisory personnel. Divers expect to dive for fun; they can learn in-depth emergency procedures from a qualified Instructor in a PADI Rescue Diver course.

As Divemaster you should always inform divers what your role will entail *during the dive.* Often the Divemaster remains on shore because this usually affords him the greatest degree of control with a large group. Under some circumstances, however, the Divemaster may wish to dive with the group. This decision is usually dependent upon depth considerations, the nature of the dive and the experience level of the divers. If you decide to participate in the dive, you have several positioning options. While in the water you may wish to *lead* the dive, remain *below* the divers or *follow* unobtrusively behind the group. In-water positioning will be

Figure 3-17
In the briefing, the Divemaster
should clearly explain what his
role will be during the dive.

discussed in greater detail later in this text.

You should consider concluding your dive briefing with an *overall* "difficulty rating" of the dive site. This rating can simply be a scale of *novice, experienced* or *advanced.* If you are accurate in your rating, you will give divers a clearer perspective of the site. In situations where divers are uncertain about the dive, this rating technique is often all that is necessary to help the diver make his decision to dive.

Pre-Dive Safety Check

Unfortunately, talking to divers may not be enough contact to ensure their safety. The Divemaster has to take some overt

Figure 3-18
A thorough pre-dive safety check is
one way to ensure that divers enter
the water in a safe, efficient manner.

action to see that divers enter the water prepared and properly equipped.

As divers ready themselves to enter the water, you should position yourself at the entry area. From this position you can easily accomplish an extensive yet quick pre-dive safety check. So you won't forget any vital portion of the pre dive check, use the helpful memory device, *Begin With Review And Friend.* This device makes it easy to remember the following:

Figure 3-19
Often, divers forget to connect low-pressure inflator hoses.

Figure 3-20
Overweighting is a common problem.

Figure 3-21
Confirm that air is turned on completely.

1. *B* (BCD) — Confirm that the low-pressure inflator is connected and that the vest contains a sufficient amount of air to enable the diver to float on the surface after entry.

2. *W* (weights) — Verify that the diver is wearing the appropriate amount of weight for the specific diving situation. Overweighting is especially common.

3. *R* (releases) — Confirm that the diver is wearing buckles that function properly and that are accessible and unhindered by other equipment.

4. *A* (air) — Confirm that the diver's tank is full and that the valve is turned on *completely.*

5. *F* (final OK) — Instruct the divers to don their fins, place their regulators in their mouths and enter the water. Once the divers enter the water, direct them to swim away from the immediate entry area.

This safety exercise may at first seem unreasonably extensive and time-consuming, but with practice you can complete it with great efficiency and go nearly unnoticed by the divers. It is helpful to have additional supervisory personnel on hand to assist you with pre-dive safety checks.

Accounting Procedures

When supervising only a few divers, the Divemaster may actually be able to lead the group during the dive. When it is impractical or impossible to supervise the group while diving, you should remain out of the water and in a position that will offer the best vantage point of the dive site. In the latter situation, accounting procedures become particularly important, and you must use a system that will unequivocally determine each diver's status. The accounting procedure you use must be simple to administer so you won't cause needless delay or diver resentment. Regardless of the system you choose, it must provide the following information to your supervisory personnel:

1. The name of *every* diver involved in the activity
2. Buddy-team assignments
3. The time of entry and exit
4. Dive-profile information that includes maximum depth, bottom time and surface interval for each dive

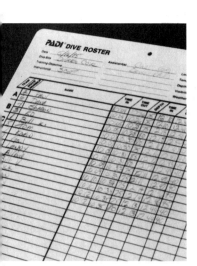

Figure 3-22
Using the PADI Dive Roster is the perfect way to assure that all pertinent information is recorded.

The Divemaster or other supervisory personnel must be available to check each diver in and out of the water. Check the status of your dive roster between each dive and at the conclusion of the final dive to confirm that everyone is safely out of the water. The PADI Dive Roster is an excellent tool to facilitate accounting procedures. This durable plastic roster provides a place for all vital information.

Dive-Supervision Procedures

The procedures for supervising divers varies according to whether the supervision will be done in or out of the water. Therefore, out-of-water supervision techniques will be discussed separately from in-water techniques. Generally, the guidelines for maintaining adequate diver supervision remain the same regardless of the environment in which divers are being supervised. These guidelines include:

1. Proper vantage point
2. Appropriate equipment
3. Readiness for response

Out-of-Water Supervision

As we stated earlier, when the group size exceeds that which the Divemaster can easily manage while in the water, someone (usually the Divemaster) must remain out of the water in a supervisory capacity. Such out-of-water supervision is

Figure 3-23
Out-of-water supervision is
most effective when conducted
through constant surveillance
from a high vantage point.

essential to being prepared for any emergencies that may arise. When you are supervising on the surface, your role is to maintain constant visual surveillance, to coordinate all activities and, if necessary, to direct emergency procedures.

It is difficult for you to maintain adequate surveillance of the dive site if you are not positioned in the proper manner or location. Usually, it is best to position yourself close to the water if the dive is taking place from the shore, but, depending upon the circumstances involved, it may be necessary to position yourself on higher ground to obtain the best vantage point. You may also want to consider positioning yourself at an area where you anticipate problems, rather than at the entry/exit point. In some unusual cases, more than one out-of-water supervisor may be required to maintain adequate supervision.

As we discussed earlier, there are certain equipment items that will make it easier to supervise the dive site. When considering such items, the Divemaster should take his personal comfort into account, as well. Because supervision usually requires little energy to be expended, you should dress appropriately for the conditions under which you will be supervising. In colder weather, warm clothes (including a windbreaker) are essential; whereas warmer, sunny weather requires sun protection and dehydration prevention. Sunglasses should be considered standard in all types of weather.

Figure 3-24
In the event of an emergency,
someone designated as a responder
should be constantly prepared
to enter the water immediately.

Probably the most overlooked aspect of out-of-water supervision is *readiness for response*. The primary function of supervision is to provide assistance to divers, if necessary. If the Divemaster is not prepared to provide that assistance, supervision has no value. Diving supervision is *not* complete unless a means for rendering *immediate* assistance to divers in need is provided.

The equipment items and supervisory personnel needed to provide aid are dependent on the locale and nature of the dive. For this reason it may seem difficult to determine just what *is* necessary. Actually, there are several considerations that remain constant, regardless of the circumstances.

Should an emergency arise and aid is needed, someone should be available to enter the water immediately and have all necessary equipment available to him. This person is called the *responder*, and you should designate someone for this role prior to each dive. Depending on the dive site and weather conditions, the responder may have to make special equipment considerations to be ready for an emergency. Diving in cold water, for example, requires the responder to wear at least an exposure suit at all times and be able to don the remaining equipment quickly.

It is unfortunate that out-of-water supervision is often left to unqualified individuals who happen to be on hand. Such an apathetic approach is unacceptable. Out-of-water supervision requires trained personnel and the same high degree of planning as in-water supervision. Dive supervision, whether in or out of the water, should be left in the hands of a qualified Divemaster.

In-Water Supervision

In-water supervision should be considered when: 1) the group is small enough and environmental conditions are favorable to enable everyone to dive together in a single group or 2) there are already enough supervisory personnel on hand to allow adequate surface supervision. *(In-water supervision should not be attempted in lieu of surface supervision if more than one group of divers is involved with the activity.)*

Remember that *in-water* supervision does not always mean *underwater* supervision. In many cases where surface supervision is called for, the Divemaster may elect to actually position himself in the water so that he may respond more quickly. In these circumstances, you should wear the proper exposure protection and be equipped with at least a mask, fins, snorkel and BCD. A rescue board is extremely useful as a surface support station and in maintaining a higher vantage point when supervising from the surface.

Once you decide to dive *with* the group, be sure you carefully consider your positioning relative to the other divers. Underwater positioning is especially crucial because it will have a direct bearing on your vantage point, the effec-

Figure 3-25
In-water supervision can often be accomplished from the surface.

tiveness of your communications and your readiness for response.

The way in which the Divemaster should position himself is dependent, to an extent, on the experience and familiarity levels of the other divers in the group. Maintaining good underwater positioning when diving with only one or two others is easy, but supervising more than two divers is somewhat more difficult and requires that you consider four important factors.

1. Identify the diver(s) most likely to have a problem.
2. Determine *where* a problem is likely to occur.
3. Determine the effects of environmental conditions.
4. Establish the function of the Divemaster.

By asking four simple questions, you can easily obtain the information you need to maintain effective positioning

Figure 3-26
In determining his location for underwater supervision, the Divemaster should select a position near the area of greatest potential danger.

with the group. These questions include the following:

Which diver is most likely to experience difficulty? Here, the considerations discussed in "Dive Planning" regarding diver assessment are important. Only through careful diver assessment can this question be answered. Your positioning should obviously be proximate to the diver most expected to experience difficulty.

At what point or location will problems be most likely? Answering this question requires careful environmental considerations. Entries and exits are often problematic; surf presents its own particular problems; and diving near underwater walls or abrupt drop-offs provides yet another set of unique problems. Because it is impossible for you to be in all places at all times, concentrate your efforts on the most probable locations for problems to arise. Generally, you should position yourself *between* the divers and the probable location of any difficulties.

What will be the effects of environmental conditions? An adequate environmental assessment conducted prior to the dive should easily answer this question. Factors like visibility, current and surface conditions will often determine, more than any other factor, where you should position yourself. Environmental conditions also determine the manageable size of the group to be supervised.

What is the function of the Divemaster during the dive? Your role and the nature of the dive will have great impact on positioning. If you are to serve as a "tour guide," then the

Figure 3-27
When functioning as an underwater "tour guide," the Divemaster should concentrate on keeping the group together.

only logical position for you to assume is the lead. On the other hand, if your role is simply to ensure the divers' safety while they direct their own dive, then a more unobtrusive position behind the divers may be in order. Regardless of your position, however, the pace of the dive should be appro priate to the abilities and desires of the divers. After all, you ar there for the convenience of the divers, not vice versa.

Emergency Procedures

The most important emergency procedures to the Divemaster are *buddy separation, out-of-air emergencies* and *recall procedures.* Buddy-separation problems will be significantly decreased if you review the procedures covered in the previous segment on The Dive Briefing with the divers in the group prior to the dive.

You may easily avoid out-of-air emergencies in the grouj by *constantly* watching the divers' submersible pressure gauges (SPGs). In fact, monitoring the air supply of divers should be one of the your major duties while under water. If

Figure 3-28
When supervising under water, a primary function of the Divemaster is monitoring divers' air supplies.

an emergency should still occur, you must be able to handle the situation. Emergency situations will require you to be competent in all forms of dependent emergency ascents (buddy breathing and alternate air source), and for this reason, all Divemasters should always carry some form of ar alternate air source.

When you are supervising the group under water, recall procedures are easy because you have only to gain the divers' attention. When supervising on the surface however, recalling submerged divers is more difficult. Submerged divers may be recalled with audible signals, such as those emitted by striking a metal object (like a tank) under water or by activating a specially designed underwater-communication/recall system.

Most of the problems associated with emergencies can

be adequately handled through proper communications prior to the dive. This is why communications and emergency procedures are to be considered vital parts of the dive briefing.

Environmental Orientation Dives

Because divers are usually trained in one specific type of environment, problems may occur when they dive for the first time in an environment that is different than the one in which they were trained. A diver who was trained in a quarry making his first tropical ocean dive is an example of a potentially troublesome situation. To help divers overcome their difficulties in such transitions, it is suggested that you give them a formal orientation to any area that is new to them.

In the interest of promoting this safety concept to the diving public, PADI officially sanctions and provides recognition for those who complete an *Environmental Orientation Dive.* PADI Divemaster Members (who are insured and renewed) are fully sanctioned to conduct these dives.

An Environmental Orientation dive may be conducted for *any* certified diver. The requirements do *not* include any diving-skills assessment, but should instead include a thorough pre-dive briefing covering the following:

1. An area overview stressing any information relative

Figure 3-29
A PADI Environmental Orientation dive is a superb way of acquainting divers with new areas and techniques.

to safety or to important aspects of the environment that could affect diver performance.

2. Information on specialized equipment or techniques related to the dive. Of particular importance are entries and exits appropriate for the locale.

3. Information related to local regulations, ordinances or standards of practice, such as game laws or appropriate diver etiquette.

4. Orientation information indicating the locations of various diving-related services, such as professional dive stores, air stations or charter boats.

During the Environmental Orientation dive, the Divemaster acts as a type of tour guide, diving with the individual and providing any needed assistance. When the dive is over, you should conduct a thorough debriefing with

Figure 3-30
During a PADI Environmental Orientation dive emphasis should be placed on any information or technique that is unique to the area.

the diver, reviewing any significant events, problems or questions. Finally, encourage the diver to log the dive and then make sure you sign his log book. Often, Divemasters will purchase customized rubber stamps (self-inking are best) containing their names and PADI numbers for use in verifying log books. Many divers find this type of entry in their log books particularly desirable as additional verification of their diving experiences.

The diver may then be provided with a decal that affixes to their certification card as recognition for completing an Environmental Orientation dive. There are three types of orientation decals available from PADI:

Figure 3-31
The Divemaster should make it a practice to sign divers' log books at the conclusion of the dive.

1. *Green* — Indicates a dive made in a freshwater environment.

2. *Blue* — Indicates a dive made in an ocean environment with water temperatures of 40-70°F/4-21°C.

3. *Red* — Indicates a dive made in an ocean environment with water temperatures above 70°F/21°C.

Figure 3-32
Divers who complete a PADI Environmental Orientation dive should immediately be issued the appropriate decal.

Note: The year in which the dive was made is also indicated on the decal. PADI requires no other registration procedure.

PADI Divemaster Members are highly encouraged to use this popular, valuable program to promote diver safety and to provide incentive for individuals to dive with qualified supervisory personnel. Remember, however, that this program is an orientation and *not* an assessment of diving ability.

Summary

In this section we discussed, in a general sense, what are probably the most important aspects of being a Divemaster. Much of this information will be applied to more specific circumstances in later sections. The essence of what we presented here involved the management and control of diving activities, from the Divemaster's perspective. We very specifically defined the term *control* and determined that it requires the elements of *preparation, communication, positioning* and *recognition*.

We also discussed the *equipment* required for effective dive control and its use, before turning to an in-depth discussion of the *dive briefing*. The dive briefing was explained as consisting of an extensive *area orientation* and *pre-dive safety check*. Guidelines for setting up an *accounting procedure* were then presented.

We presented extensive information on *dive-supervision procedures,* both in and out of water. We determined that adequate supervision requires the Divemaster to consider the proper *vantage point, appropriate equipment* and *readiness for response.* We detailed various emergency procedures and concluded with a discussion of the PADI Environmental Orientation dive program.

In this section we also assumed a diving scenario that did not involve training activities. In the next section, we will discuss the Divemaster's role during training activities.

Name _____

Date _____

Knowledge Review
Dive Management and Control

1. Define the term *control* as it relates to dive supervision and list the essential elements of control.

_____

_____

_____

_____

2. List and briefly explain six items of equipment that are useful in the management and control of large-scale diving activities.

_____

_____

_____

_____

3. Within the dive briefing, what information should be presented by the Divemaster concerning the *area orientation?*

_____

_____

_____

_____

4. Within the dive briefing, what information should be presented by the Divemaster concerning the *pre-dive safety check?*

_____

_____

_____

_____

5. What specific information should be included in any accounting procedure designed to keep track of divers?

_____

_____

_____

_____

6. What are the general guidelines the Divemaster should use in planning for effective in-water and out-of-water supervision?

_____

_____

_____

_____

7. What aspect of out-of-water supervision is most often overlooked? What factors are essential in assuring that this vital aspect of supervision is adequately fulfilled?

_____

_____

_____

_____

8. In-water supervision of divers should be considered _only_ when certain conditions exist; what are those conditions? When should in-water supervision _not_ be attempted?

_____

_____

_____

_____

9. State the four considerations that should guide the Divemaster in determining where and how to position himself during the in-water supervision of a dive.

_____

_____

_____

_____

10. In terms of supervising others, which emergency procedures are of prime importance to the Divemaster? What steps can the Divemaster take to help avoid these problems?

_____

_____

_____

_____

11. Who is qualified to conduct PADI Environmental Orientation dives? What prerequisites must a diver possess in order to participate in this program?

_____

_____

_____

_____

12. Explain the color-coding system of the PADI Environmental Orientation dive decals that are affixed to the diver's certification card.

Green: _____

Blue: _____

Red: _____

Four

Supervising Students In Training

Section Objectives

☐ Explain the role and responsibility of the Divemaster as prescribed for PADI training activities at all levels.

☐ Define the terms *professionalism* and *proper attitude* and explain their importance regarding student development.

☐ Describe several techniques useful in the control of student divers in both pool and open-water environments.

☐ List several common problems encountered in pool and open-water skill performance and describe the means to overcome and prevent these problems.

☐ Explain what training activities PADI prescribes for the development of the Divemaster's knowledge, awareness and experience concerning diver/student supervision and problem recognition.

Introduction

As noted in Course Orientation and the Role of the Divemaster, the PADI Divemaster rating qualifies an individual for membership in the PADI Association. This membership entitles the Divemaster to certain privileges and duties, many of which are related to the training of student divers. Unlike any other section of this manual, *this* section deals with these unique training-related considerations.

Divemaster involvement in student training is essential to the optimum level of success of the PADI diver training program. You are an essential member of an instructional *team* of which the instructor is the captain. In all situations where students are not under the direct observation of a cer-

Figure 4-1
The Divemaster is a vital member of an instructional team of which the instructor is the captain.

tified instructor, the responsibility for their supervision falls to you. No other duty is more important than your role as an instructional assistant.

A clear distinction must be made between the duties of the Divemaster and those of the instructor. Only a certified PADI Instructor is qualified to independently *teach* scuba training activities. Your duties are restricted to the *supervision* of student divers and *assisting* the instructor. This section will provide details on how you may accomplish these duties.

The Divemaster as an Instructional Assistant

The function of the Divemaster during training activities may be varied, but generally, it involves providing an increased level of safety and comfort to those in training. Your role will also be dependent upon the environment in which the training takes place, and the level of training being conducted.

As indicated earlier, your primary role is to provide supervision for those not under direct instructor observation. This is especially important with entry-level Open Water Diver students, as these individuals are not yet certified.

*Figure 4-2
A primary role of the Divemaster
is supervising student training
activities, both in the pool...*

Conversely, because of their experience level, students enrolled in Continuing Education courses do not require the same degree of control. However, you must never assume that *all* Continuing Education students are adequately experienced. Even divers with substantial numbers of dives to their credit may not have experience in the particular activity or location in which a course is being conducted. Another consideration is that a successful Continuing Education course often recruits students *directly* out of entry-level courses, and thus these individuals may have had no more than four or five previous dives. All of these situations point to the need for thorough diver assessment prior to any Continuing Education training activity.

As the Divemaster and the instructor are members of the same team, it is part of the Divemaster's duty to provide the instructor with information concerning student performance. Often, you will see students under different conditions and circumstances than the instructor; and often a different type of rapport develops between you and the students. This unique relationship can provide an excellent insight into stu-

*Figure 4-3
...and in open water.*

dent attitude and performance. A well-trained Divemaster is invaluable in the development of competent divers because you are a "second pair of eyes" for the instructor.

The Divemaster will also be called on to handle logistical matters, such as equipment dispersal or other preparatory activities. This should not be looked upon as busywork because performing these duties enables you to gain an understanding of the complete nature of the instructor's job. Remember that a primary goal of Divemaster training is to provide adequate preparation for becoming an instructor; not all of what an instructor does involves teaching.

Another duty of the Divemaster is somewhat indirect, yet no less important. You are a role model for student divers. Whether this duty will result in a positive or negative effect will depend upon your attitude and professionalism.

Figure 4-4
For the instructor, the Divemaster is an important source of input on student attitude and performance.

Figure 4-5
Often the Divemaster is responsible for the logistical support of training activities.

This role-model function carries with it a heavy responsibility for you to conduct yourself in an exemplary manner at all times. When dealing with students, you must realize that you can no longer be concerned with only yourself. One's behavior both while in an official capacity and while off duty will set an important example for others and can significantly affect your credibility.

The Certified Assistant

The term *certified assistant* is a special status granted to PADI Divemasters and relates to their role during student training activities. Only PADI Divemasters, PADI Assistant Instructors and PADI Instructors qualify for this status.

Certified assistants have a vital role within the PADI System because they, and only they, are qualified to guide student divers on experience tours in the training area under the general supervision of an instructor.

An important qualification to this procedure is, however, that during the Open Water Diver course, Divemaster escorted tours may take place only after students have completed all skills evaluations with a qualified PADI Instructor. In addi-

Figure 4-6
As a Certified Assistant,
the Divemaster is qualified
to conduct experience tours
with divers who have completed
skills evaluation with an instructor.

tion, a Divemaster may *not* independently supervise the tour for experience during Open Water Training Dive No.1. Only a certified PADI Instructor is qualified to supervise this first experience tour. When conducting independent experience tours during Open Water Training Dives 2-5, PADI Standards stipulate that the Divemaster supervise not more than two students at a time. This ratio changes when supervising students in a Continuing Education course. You should refer to the PADI *Instructor Manual* for details on supervising Continuing Education training activities. These ratios apply, however, only to very favorable conditions. Rough, turbid or very cold water requires reduced ratios for student safety.

In this sense, *general* supervision with regard to the instructor may mean that although he is present and in control of the dive site, he may not need to personally accompany the Divemaster and the tour group. An important qualification to this procedure is, however, that during entry-level training (Basic Diver and Open Water Diver), these tours may take place only after students have completed all skill evaluations for that dive with a certified PADI Instructor.

Taking responsibility for students who are not yet fully trained is a considerable one; it is *the* most important and fundamental distinction between the Divemaster and other levels of PADI diver certifications.

Professionalism and Attitude

As we implied in the previous segment, the Divemaster's professionalism and attitude have great impact on student development. The importance of having a high degree of professionalism and having the proper attitude cannot be overstated. With such significance ascribed to these areas, it is necessary to define and explore more fully what is meant by *professionalism* and *attitude*.

Professionalism

The term *professionalism* is often used without regard for its meaning. The PADI Divemaster rating is a professional level of certification, and an understanding of this word is in order. To fulfill the definition of professionalism, one must fulfill five interdependent, essential criteria.

A professional must possess *specialized expertise.* The content and structure of the PADI Divemaster course is meticulously designed to take this consideration into account. Thus, completion of the PADI Divemaster course virtually assures you that you will possess the necessary expertise required to be a professional.

Figure 4-7
Professionalism *requires a high degree of specialized expertise.*

A professional is one who follows a *prescribed standard of practice.* PADI Standards are designed with the utmost consideration for diver safety and sound educational practice. Adherence to these standards is vital to the development of a safe diver and for liability protection as well. Other standards of practice, as exemplified in the PADI Safe Diving Practices Statement of Understanding, are a result of years of experience. Whether acting in an official capacity or not, the Divemaster has a moral and legal duty to abide by these standards of his profession.

Professionalism requires that one *remain up-to-date* with the state of the art in his chosen profession. Information and techniques within all professions are in a continual state of growth. To refuse to or to make no effort to stay current is simply irresponsible and unprofessional. You as Divemaster should take advantage of the opportunities that PADI and other sources provide for updating. PADI publications, workshops, courses and Professional Development Seminars are a few of the options at your disposal.

As a key member of the instructional team, a high degree of trust will be placed in the Divemaster both by the instructor and the students. Your conduct will have significant impact on the credibility and effectiveness of the instructional program. You must always treat students fairly

Figure 4-8
As a professional, the Divemaster must remain up-to-date with the latest ideas and techniques in diving.

Figure 4-9
In addition to conveying a professional appearance, students will also expect the Divemaster to act ethically and objectively.

and without the appearance of favoritism or prejudice. In this regard, *ethical and impartial conduct* are essential to the definition of professionalism.

A final aspect of professionalism is *appearance.* Nothing can destroy a professional image faster than making an improper presentation to the public. One could be the most competent Divemaster in the world, yet his effectiveness would be severely diminished by wearing a tattered T-shirt, cutoffs and dive gear that is poorly maintained and outdated. Quite simply, students will expect those in whom they place their trust to convey a professional image.

Attitude

The topic of attitude is given very little attention at most other levels of diver training. This usually causes relatively few problems because, as a diver, a poor attitude usually affects no one but that individual. At the Divemaster level, however, this situation changes considerably. Your attitude plays a more important role because you must deal with others. But what are the crucial aspects of your attitude as a Divemaster, and what expectation will be made in this regard?

As we've mentioned several times in this section, the Divemaster is a member of a *team* directed by the instructor. Just as no other team could be successful without common agreement among its members, the instructional team must be in agreement as to how the course is to be taught. The in-

Figure 4-10
To be an effective member of the instructional staff, the Divemaster must fully understand how divers are trained, and why such practices are valid.

structor has the right to expect his staff members to support his training decisions. A Divemaster who disagrees with the instructor's training approach will have nothing but a negative effect upon the training effort. Therefore, your attitude as Divemaster must *agree with the instructor and the PADI System.*

Another requirement of a proper attitude involves *accepting the need for consistency and adherence to training standards.* As a professional, the Divemaster in fact *agrees* to follow a prescribed standard. To have the proper attitude, you must also *want* to follow this standard. Consistency in training is essential for the effectiveness of learning. You cannot take it upon yourself to alter the manner or

Figure 4-11
As students will often model
their behavior after the Divemaster,
he must always adhere to proper
and safe diving practices.

technique used to teach a skill without the instructor's knowledge and permission. Additionally, any supervisory staff not adhering to the instructor's training approach will undermine the teaching effort and the credibility of the instructional/supervisory staff. And remember, the concept of adhering to safe diving standards applies to your *personal* diving activities as well as those in which you are in a supervisory capacity.

The Divemaster must want to do his job because of the satisfaction and enjoyment he receives from helping others. This idea differs fundamentally from someone who attempts a misguided ego gratification by purposely trying to make the training experience difficult and arbitrary. There is no room on a professional instructional team for this type of behavior. An attitude of *empathy and a concern for others* is an unquestionable requirement of the effective Divemaster.

Figure 4-12
Regardless of the setting,
the Divemaster's empathy and
concern for others must be
evident at all times.

A final component of a proper attitude involves the equipment-intensive nature of diving. Proper equipment makes diving safer and more enjoyable. Diver surveys and practical experience show that student divers who do not purchase the proper equipment have a higher chance of becoming diver dropouts. It is the responsibility of the instructional team — including the Divemaster — to *encourage students to acquire proper diving equipment.* This is another reason for you to use modern, well-maintained equipment.

Control Techniques

In general, a higher degree of control is necessary when dealing with students than when supervising certified divers in a recreational setting. In addition to the control techniques introduced in Dive Management and Control, there are other important considerations when dealing with student divers. One such consideration is a result of the fact that students are usually trained in a pool as well as in open water.

*Figure 4-13
When supervising students, a
higher-than-normal degree of
control and supervision is expected.*

Control in the Pool

In entry-level training, all skills are first taught in the pool or similar environment before proceeding into open water. But, the Divemaster's function is *not* to teach. Instead, your function is to supervise student practice only after the technique has been taught by a qualified instructor. After the initial instruction, you may then provide input to the instructor on student performance. You may also help maintain control by supervising equipment distribution, preparation and suit-up — especially in the early phases of training when students are unfamiliar with equipment and technique.

The Divemaster must be conscious at all times of the locations and positions of students in the pool. You should exercise great care to ensure that students are under constant supervision and that the skills are being practiced in the safest possible manner and location. Those students in deep water, particularly, require constant attention. Prior to all training sessions, instructions should be provided to the students concerning *how, when* and *where* they are to be positioned for the various training and practice activities.

Although not qualified to teach, the Divemaster must nonetheless be thoroughly familiar with the skills that are to be taught and the techniques used to teach them. You should be familiar with the skills outlined on the PADI Aquatic Cue Cards (Pool Skills), part of the PADI Modular Scuba Course. (It is suggested that all Divemaster candidates obtain these valuable training aids.) To help the instructor, you must know what the instructor is going to do. The cue cards contain valuable information including briefing and debriefing outlines for open-water training, communication and emergency procedures, and boat-diving terminology.

Often the instructor will set certain ground rules for pool activities. One of your primary functions as Divemaster is to enforce these rules to maintain control and insure student safety. Ground rules are often dependent upon the specific facility used; many facilities will *require* the enforcement of certain rules. The following are some general recommendations for all pool-training activities useful in promoting safety and proper skill development:

1. No students should be allowed in the pool without staff supervision.

2. Students should not be allowed to attempt a skill that they have not been taught. (The Divemaster must never attempt to teach in lieu of the instructor.)

3. To develop the proper habits for open-water diving, adherence to the buddy system should be required. (Provide some form of incentive for buddy-team members to maintain close proximity.)

4. Using the side of the pool for support while on the surface should not be allowed. (No pool sides will be readily available in open water.)

5. While on the surface, students should not be allowed to remove their masks unless necessary or appropriate. If

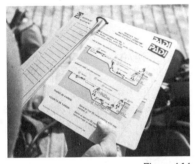

Figure 4-14
Using the PADI Aquatic Cue Cards (Pool) is an excellent way for the Divemaster to become acquainted with required pool activities.

Figure 4-15
The responsibility of strictly enforcing pool "ground rules" usually falls to the Divemaster and other instructional personnel.

masks are removed, they should *not* be placed on the forehead. (Removing the mask in times of stress is an important habit to break.)

Teaching diving in the pool is an attempt to simulate the open-water environment. Therefore, the same control techniques you will use in open water should be implemented in the pool in order for students to become accustomed to your supervisory role.

Control in Open Water

In addition to in-water supervision, adequate *surface* supervision is essential to maintaining control of all but the smallest classes. With larger classes, a Divemaster should be in overall charge of the logistics of the training site. This will allow the instructor to concentrate fully upon the evaluation of student performance. You may supervise suiting up (particularly in the later phases of training); check-in and check-

Figure 4-16
Simulating the reality of an open-water training dive is an extremely effective way of preparing students while simultaneously reducing their anxiety.

Figure 4-17
With larger classes, a Divemaster
is often assigned the duty of
onshore activities supervisor.

out procedures; entries and exits; and may assist handling problems that may arise on the surface. Only in classes small enough to allow the instructor to dive with the entire group should surface supervision be considered optional.

When in the water, the Divemaster's function is to supervise the students — particularly those who are not under direct observation of the instructor. While the same elements of control that we identified in the section on Dive Management and Control — preparation, communication, positioning and recognition — apply to students as well as other divers, some of these elements require closer consideration when viewed in a training context.

When working with students, *positioning* becomes more crucial than when supervising recreational activities. Generally, the Divemaster should maintain a closer proximity to the students than he may in other situations. Staying close is especially important with entry-level students who have had little or no previous experience. Even though the instructor may have only a small group when evaluating student skills, he must nonetheless divert attention from some students to concentrate on others. The effective Divemaster is conscious of this and will continually change position as necessary to more closely supervise those whom the instructor cannot. The students should also be encouraged to maintain awareness of the Divemaster while the instructor's attention is diverted.

Your *problem-recognition* skills also become more important with students in open water. You may expect a higher occurrence of problems when dealing with students because they have little experience and their anxiety levels

Figure 4-18
When dealing with students,
skills related to problem recognition become increasingly important.

are often high. Student divers will typically make mistakes
that would be considered unlikely for experienced divers,
and the Divemaster must be aware of and anticipate this
possibility at all times.

Your expectations of a student's performance may vary
from one individual to another, and you need to be able to
identify individuals while under water. This can be relatively
simple if students are wearing different types of equipment.
If the majority of the class is using similar rental equipment,
however, problems in establishing their identities while
under water will develop. To overcome this problem, arm
bands, color-coded hoods or other easily identifiable equipment may be used. The students should also be able to identify the staff, particularly in the event of a problem.

Figure 4-19
The Divemaster must conduct
an especially thorough pre-dive
safety check when supervising
uncertified student divers.

Commonly Encountered Problems

Problem recognition begins with being aware of what problems typically occur with student divers. The most common problems encountered in both the pool and open water are predictable. There are two important aspects of problem recognition: 1) *proper response* should a problem arise and 2) *prevention* of the problem. Although knowing how to properly respond to problems is essential, it is more important for you to develop the ability to prevent problems from occurring.

Figure 4-20
Most of the commonly encountered problems are easily antcipated and can be solved through preventative measures.

Typical Pool Problems

In the Pool Skills and Common Problems chart, the major skills required in each of the five confined-water sessions of the PADI Modular Scuba Course and related problems are listed. For each of the problems described, you should consider what appropriate action may be taken to overcome the problem. Next, you should review the list and determine how the problem may be *prevented* entirely. This exercise will better prepare you for your role as an instructional assistant.

Pool Skills and Common Problems

Module I

1. Equipment preparation/assembly
   - improper adjustment
   - inattentive student
   - tank allowed to stand unattended

2. Donning scuba and weights (while standing in shallow end)
   - backpack or BCD impeding function/position of weight belt
   - trapping hoses under backpack or weight belt straps

3. BCD inflation/deflation
   - unable to inflate vest
   - unable to deflate vest
   - gross overinflation

4. Regulator recovery/clear
   - not exhaling while regulator is out of mouth
   - unable to locate/reach regulator second stage
   - choking on water

5. Mask clearing
   - inability to exhale through nose while submerged
   - improper head position (not looking up)
   - mask separated too far from face during exhalation

6. Use of fins
   - too much knee-bending while swimming
   - student complains of "cramps"

7. Equalizing/underwater swimming
   - equalizing too late/descending too fast
   - unable to adequately grasp nose through mask
   - wandering off from group

8. Ascents and descents
   - not maintaining position near buddy
   - not checking time
   - not watching where they are going

(Continued)

Pool Skills and Common Problems

(Continued)

Module II

9. Controlled seated entry
   - loss of balance
   - unable to push off from pool side

10. Snorkel clearing (blast method)
    - unable to exhale quickly or forcefully enough
    - poor airway control (coughing or choking)

11. Scuba/snorkel exchange
    - poor airway control
    - improper positioning of snorkel

12. No mask breathing
    - holding nose
    - unable to prevent inhalation through nose

13. Deep water exit
    - removing tank before weights
    - dropping weight belt
    - unsecure weights slipping off belt

14. Donning scuba (while standing on pool deck)
    - no buddy assistance
    - not conducting pre-dive safety drill
    - hoses trapped under waist strap

15. Giant stride entry
    - not holding mask during entry
    - insufficient air in BCD
    - not signaling "OK" or swimming away from entry area

Module III

16. No-mask swimming
    - running into others or pool sides
    - getting away from group
    - water up the nose

17. Mask scramble
    - loss of control

18. Neutral buoyancy (fin pivot)
    - adding too much air to BCD
    - holding breath

19. Alternate air source use
    - lack of secure hold between buddies
    - buoyancy problems

20. Free-flow regulator breathing
    - not pushing the purge valve hard or long enough
    - not allowing air to escape around mouthpiece

21. Emergency Swimming Ascent
    - no continuous exhalation/sound
    - ascending too fast/slow
    - not looking up while ascending

Module IV

22. Headfirst surface dive (skin diving)
    - too buoyant/negative
    - swimming with arms

23. Displacement snorkel clearing
    - begin exhalation too soon
    - not looking up during ascent

24. Neutral buoyant (hovering)
    - diver unaware of ascent
    - kicking to maintain position

25. Buddy breathing
    - improper/inadequate hand signals
    - not exhaling between breaths
    - too much time between breaths

Module V

26. Weight belt removal/replacement (surface and under water)
    - not pulling belt away from body
    - dropping belt or insecure weight
    - unable to manipulate belt by feel alone

27. Tank removal/replacement (surface and under water)
    - entangling snorkel with backpack strap
    - dislodging mask
    - entangling BCD hose
    - accidently removing weight belt

Typical Open Water Problems

Many of the problems students encounter in open water are the same as those encountered in the pool. There are some problems, however, that are different or unique to a particular environment.

The Open Water Skills and Common Problems Chart lists the skills required for certification as a PADI Open Water Diver and the common problems associated with each skill. As with the previous segment on pool skills, you should review the chart considering both how to prevent and overcome the problems described.

Open Water Skills and Common Problems

1. Equipment preparation
   - malfunctioning or missing equipment
   - improper assembly of tank/BCD
   - rocking boat

2. Suiting up
   - overheating
   - impeded or inaccessible buckles
   - no buddy assistance

3. Entry
   - one buddy prepared to enter water, other not
   - no air in BCD
   - struggling on surface
   - air not turned on

4. Buoyancy check
   - exhaustion/apprehension
   - too buoyant/negative

5. Controlled descent
   - cannot equalize
   - drifts away from group/buddy
   - sinks out of control
   - cannot locate regulator
   - refuses to descend

6. Buoyancy control (fin pivot)
   - silting of bottom (excessive movement)
   - insufficient weight
   - holding breath to stabilize buoyancy
   - ascending out of control or unaware of ascent

7. Regulator recovery and clear
   - holding breath while regulator is out of mouth
   - panic once regulator is removed
   - unable to find regulator once removed

8. Mask clear and removal
   - shock of cold/salty water contacting face
   - water going up nose
   - panic/attempting to ascend
   - hood/hair prevents mask from sealing

9. Alternate air source use (stationary and ascending)
   - sand/mud in spare regulator
   - unable to locate spare regulator
   - regulator accidently pulled from receiver's mouth
   - spare second stage donned upside down
   - buoyancy problems

10. Free descent with reference
    - descending too fast
    - unable to equalize
    - drifting away from group/buddy

11. Buoyancy control (oral inflation)
    - lips too cold to seal around mouthpiece
    - unable to locate regulator between breaths

12. Underwater tour
    - buddy/group separation
    - swimming too fast/slow
    - not following directions
    - excessive breathing/exhaustion

13. Surface swimming with compass
    - looking at destination instead of course
    - lack of buddy awareness
    - swimming too fast

14. Free descent without reference
    - refusal to descend
    - descending too quickly or out of control
    - unable to equalize
    - buddy/group separation   *(Continued)*

Open Water Skills and Common Problems

(Continued)

15. Buddy breathing (stationary and ascending)
    - inadequate contact between buddies
    - not exhaling between breaths
    - failure to control buoyancy during ascent

16. Removal and replacement of scuba on the surface
    - student unaware of current
    - releasing weight belt instead of BCD belt
    - hoses caught under waist strap after donning

17. Underwater navigation
    - watching buddy instead of compass
    - improper positioning of compass
    - grossly off course

18. Neutral buoyancy (hovering)
    - too far from supervision
    - kicking to maintain position
    - loss of balance

19. Emergency Swimming Ascent
    - ascending too fast/slow
    - regulator out of mouth
    - not making continuous sound

20. General problems
    - mask on forehead
    - climbing onto surface float
    - not monitoring air supply
    - vertigo
    - moving away from group/buddy
    - not returning/acknowledging hand signals
    - not watching instructor
    - snorkel or regulator not in place while on surface

Figure 4-21
An important phase of the Divemaster's training is those activities in which he participates to gain insight into the diver-training process.

Divemaster Training Activities

The PADI Divemaster course is designed to provide the Divemaster with thorough training and to prepare him for his role as an instructional assistant. To accomplish this, all PADI Divemaster candidates must complete either an internship with a qualified PADI Instructor or other training activities designed for this purpose.

The internship involves the Divemaster candidate serving as an instructional assistant to a PADI Instructor for at least ten open-water training dives and five confined-water (pool) sessions. During each session in which the Divemaster candidate participates, the Instructor will complete a PADI Divemaster Program Internship Evaluation Form that enables him to determine an objective grade for the Divemaster candidate's water skills, organizational ability and attitude. A total score of 45 out of 70 points is required for the Divemaster candidate to pass the training session successfully.

The Divemaster candidate may also participate in specific practical training activities designed to increase knowledge, awareness and experience in diver/student supervision and problem recognition. The course instructor may also elect to combine this second training option with a limited internship experience. For more details on this aspec

Figure 4-22
As a result of PADI Divemaster Training, you will come to understand and anticipate the behavior of student divers.

Figure 4-23
All Divemaster candidates should acquire a copy of the latest PADI Instructor Manual for review.

of Divemaster training, consult the "PADI Divemaster Course Instructor Guide."

Summary

This section is particularly significant because it deals with possibly the most important function of the Divemaster — supervising students in training. We stressed that only a certified instructor has the qualifications to teach; the role of the Divemaster is to *supervise.* The term *certified assistant* was explained with regard to how it applies to PADI diver training and the Divemaster when he is fulfilling this role.

We detailed the importance of professionalism and attitude when dealing with students and described what is expected of the Divemaster in this regard. The requirements of professionalism were defined as: possessing a *specialized expertise;* adhering to a *prescribed standard;* remaining *up-to-date* with state-of-the art diving techniques; *ethical* and *impartial* conduct; and *proper appearance.* Proper attitude requires a philosophical agreement with the instructor and the PADI System, developing empathy and concern for others, and encouraging students to acquire proper, sufficient equipment.

From the general aspects of professionalism and attitude, we focused on the specifics of controlling students in the pool and open water. We concluded that some of the guidelines for supervising divers is also applicable to supervising students.

Problems that are commonly encountered in the pool

Figure 4-24
Unlike supervising purely recreational dives, dealing with student divers requires special attention and considerable insight.

and open-water environments were examined. The two most important aspects of problem recognition — *proper response* in the event the problem occurs and *prevention* of the problem altogether — were detailed. We concluded with a discussion of the training requirements PADI prescribes to develop the Divemaster candidate's knowledge, awareness and experience regarding diver/student supervision and problem recognition.

Proper diver education is a team effort, and as Divemaster, you are an integral member of this professional team. Only with a thorough understanding of the material presented in this section can you expect to adequately fulfill your function as an instructional assistant.

Name _____

Date _____

Knowledge Review
Supervising Students In Training

1. Contrast in general the duties of the Divemaster from those of the instructor.

_____

_____

_____

_____

2. What are the primary functions of the Divemaster as they relate to diver-training activities?

_____

_____

_____

_____

3. According to PADI Standards*, what is a *certified assistant?* What duties may this individual perform?

_____

_____

_____

*Refers to the "Standards and Procedures" section of the Instructor Manual.

4. What are the requirements of *professionalism?*

_____

_____

_____

_____

5. Explain the meaning of *proper attitude* as it pertains to the Divemaster's involvement in training activities.

_____

_____

_____

_____

6. What is the Divemaster's function with regard to pool-training activities?

_____

_____

_____

_____

7. During open-water training, describe how the Divemaster may function as a surface supervisor.

_____

_____

_____

_____

8. Why is *positioning* a particularly important element of control in dealing with student divers? How may this affect the way the Divemaster supervises students?

_____

_____

_____

_____

9. Why is *problem recognition* a particularly important element of control in dealing with student divers? How may this affect the way the Divemaster supervises students?

_____

_____

_____

_____

10. What are the two aspects of problem recognition?

_____

_____

_____

_____

Five

Boat Diving Supervision and Control

Section Objectives

☐ Describe the types of vessels used for boat-diving activities and explain what factors determine the type of vessel used in particular area or environment.

☐ Explain both the legal and general safety requirements for a diving vessel.

☐ Demonstrate basic seamanship procedures, including a general familiarity with: reading charts, hazards at sea, marine-radio operations and anchoring/docking procedures.

☐ List the important topics to be contained in a pre-dive orientation to a boat dive.

☐ Explain the essential management and control procedures relating to pre-dive, in-water and post-dive activities for boat diving.

☐ Describe several techniques or considerations useful in avoiding seasickness.

Figure 5-1
An effective Divemaster should have
a basic knowledge of seamanship
and boat-diving procedures.

Introduction

Diving and boating are a natural combination, and in many respects they are quite similar. Both are water-related, both are equipment-intensive and both require a degree of expertise. At some time or another, virtually all divers will dive from boats. In fact, because boat diving makes accessing dive sites so convenient, most divers *prefer* it.

Because boat diving is so popular, it is essential that the experienced diver possess adequate skills in this area. This section will not, however, teach general boat-diving procedures. This section *will* deal with the proper techniques and considerations for *supervising* boat diving. This information will be conveyed through a dive-*charter*-boat scenario, though the techniques presented will generally be applicable to most other boat-diving situations.

Assume that within this section, the diving vessel is being operated within U.S. territorial waters. Regardless of the country in which the Divemaster may operate, the following approach is still useful and valid. While the specific regulations of some countries may differ from those in the U.S., the scope of most regulations governing the operation of a vessel on navigable waters are similar. It is vitally important, however, for the Divemaster to become thoroughly

Figure 5-2
A knowledge of boating laws
and regulations is useful to
anyone responsible for supervising
boat-diving activities.

familiar with those regulations unique to his location or country — particularly if such regulations differ from those discussed in this section. You should contact the local maritime authority or Coast Guard to clarify any questions.

You must also give special consideration to your function as a crew member aboard the dive boat. This role will vary

Figure 5-3
The boat-based Divemaster will
often have the responsibility of
acting as a crew member in addition
to the responsibilities he has as a diver.

with the circumstances. On professionally-crewed charter boats, you will often have no function in the operation of the vessel. In this case, you should refrain from doing anything not related to supervising divers, unless you are asked. Occasionally, however, you *will* need to act as a crew member. Because this crew-member function may vary greatly, this section will relate to both functions — the Divemaster as a supervisor of divers and the Divemaster as a crew member of a dive boat.

Boat diving places unusual requirements on divers in general and on the Divemaster in particular. Boat diving requires that you be not only a competent diver, but a *seaman* as well. This dual role doubles the difficulty you may encounter in conducting a dive.

Types of Diving Vessels

The type of environment in which the vessel will be used and the distance to the dive site are the primary factors in determining the type of vessel used for diving activities. In locations where dive sites are distant, and travel is often

Figure 5-4
The styles and designs of
dive boats reflect the environ-
ments in which they operate.

necessary in less-than-ideal conditions, large, self-contained vessels may be needed. Most often, these vessels are of heavy displacement to provide the necessary interior room to accommodate divers and their equipment for extended periods of time.

Conversely, boats at diving resorts can operate much closer to dive sites, usually requiring only short-duration trips of no more than an hour. Without needing to accommodate divers for long periods, and usually in more calm or predictable environments, resorts typically operate smaller, more-open vessels.

The availability and size of the local diving market are other determining factors of the type of vessel required. It is difficult for operators to build and maintain boats designed solely for diving in areas without high concentrations of divers. In areas with small diving markets, the typical dive boat often does double duty as a fishing boat. This can in-

Figure 5-5
Fishing boats or other pleasure
craft are often used for diving.

convenience divers because many features that may make diving convenient — adequate boarding ladders, equipment stowage and on-board compressors — are not found on the typical fishing vessel. Areas with high diver concentrations, such as Florida and Southern California, can provide a sufficient market for large fleets of specially designed dive boats. One of the primary benefits of the continued growth of diving will be the increased technology and number of boats built exclusively for diving.

Dive Boat Safety Considerations

Boat-safety considerations fall into two categories: 1) legal requirements stipulated by the U.S. Coast Guard or other regulatory bodies; and 2) diving-related requirements. Safety considerations also involve both the *vessel* and its *operator*.

Figure 5-6
Persons operating boats for
hire must be duly licensed.

Figure 5-7
Most boats carrying more than six
passengers require special certification.

Anyone operating a motor vessel for hire in U.S. territorial waters is required by law to hold a valid U.S. Coast Guard operator's license. The type of license required is dependent upon the size of the vessel and the number of passengers carried. This requirement ensures that the person operating the vessel is competent. But, the requirements relate *only* to the operation and navigation of the boat and have nothing to do with the individual's knowledge or familiarity of diving and its related safety procedures. In many situations it will be your function to take responsibility for diving-related procedures.

The vessel itself is required to be *certified* if it is to carry more than six passengers. Certificates of inspection must be prominently displayed on the vessel. The certificate specifies the area in which the vessel may operate, the number of passengers that can be carried, minimum crew requirements and minimum lifesaving and fire-fighting equipment requirements.

It is wise to be aware of the different definitions of the term *passenger.* The Coast Guard's interpretation of passenger is *very* encompassing and is considered to be *anyone* who contributes *any form* of compensation in exchange for passage. Compensation can mean not only money, but fuel, food and so on.

Another important dive-boat safety requirement involves the role of a vessel's operator during diving activities. According to Coast Guard regulations, the boat captain must remain *on board* and *in control* of the vessel while at anchor. The captain may dive *only* if another licensed operator is on board and left in charge of the vessel.

The appropriate licenses must be displayed in a prominent area of the vessel. In situations where the Divemaster does not have a direct relationship with the vessel or its operator, he must make a thorough check to make certain that the vessel and operator fulfill all legal requirements.

Legal requirements regarding on-board equipment vary with the size and type of the vessel. Generally, all vessels must carry the following safety items:

1. *Approved* personal flotation devices (one for each person on board)
2. Fire extinguishers
3. Signaling devices (horn, bell, etc.)
4. Radio

Vessels are also required to have navigation lights and, according to the boat's size and design, may require backup fire and pollution-control systems. Certified vessels (those carrying more than six passengers) must be inspected by the Coast Guard on a regular basis. For vessels carrying less than six passengers, safety inspections are voluntary, although highly encouraged.

Other safety considerations are relevant to diving activities. Generally, there are no legal requirements made of diving vessels other than those required for all other vessels. Regardless of legal requirements, every boat from which diving activities take place should have the following equipment on board:

1. Oxygen (ideally with a delivery system capable of 100% concentrations)
2. First-aid kit
3. Appropriate dive flags
4. Stern line and float
5. Chase boat or rescue board
6. A diver-recall system

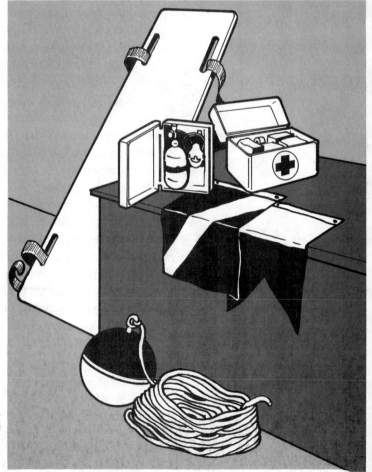

Figure 5-8
In addition to standard on-board equipment, boats involved in diving operations should also have other specialized items aboard.

Other features are important in evaluating whether fishing or pleasure craft is suitable for diving activities. One such feature is the means by which divers exit and enter the vessel. Well-constructed boarding ladders that are capable of holding fully equipped divers are rare, except on boats that regularly carry divers. Additionally, features like cutaway gunwales, which facilitate entries and exits, are rarely seen on vessels not designed or customized specifically for diving.

Figure 5-9
Special board ladders or platforms are the best means by which divers may safely enter and exit the water.

Also, consider whether the vessel has adequate space to accommodate the number of anticipated divers. A boat that will comfortably accommodate a maximum of 20 fishermen, for example, will probably be incapable of accommodating the same number of divers because of the increased amount of equipment required for diving.

In addition to the proper equipment, trained personnel are required to ensure a safely organized dive. For this reason there is no substitute for a well-trained Divemaster. However, even on larger boats (requiring more than one crew member), *all* crew should be aware of at least the rudiments of safe-diving practices and boat-diving procedures. Though it may be desirable for the captain and all other crew members to be certified divers, this may not always be the case.

Particularly when using boats and crew unaccustomed to diving, it is extremely important for the Divemaster to familiarize the captain and crew with diving-related safety procedures. Practices such as the use of the dive flag, when and when not to start the engine and entry/exit considerations must be thoroughly discussed prior to any diving activities.

Figure 5-10
An important responsibility of the Divemaster is to acquaint a captain who is unfamiliar with boat-diving operations to the proper procedures.

Finally, in addition to considering passenger safety, the Divemaster should show consideration for passenger convenience. Ideally, a dive boat should provide adequate protection from the elements, ample room to prepare for dives and rest between dives, and an adequate supply of fresh water. Other convenience items that are greatly appreciated by divers may include a cooler in which to stow beverages and food, and a freshwater shower. Though these items are not essential to diver safety, they will go a long way in helping increase diver enjoyment.

Remote Area Considerations

Occasionally, boat-diving operations occur in highly remote locations where there are few formal regulations governing the safety and operation of a dive boat (or any other type of vessel). When faced with supervising boat-diving operations

Figure 5-11
Because safety and operating regulations vary, the Divemaster must exercise great care when supervising boat-diving activities in highly remote locations.

in such an area, exercise special care and consideration.

Often, those operating vessels in remote areas are local fisherman who probably will know little about diving operations. The Divemaster is therefore responsible for filling this gap in knowledge. The boat operator and Divemaster must agree on important procedures, such as anchoring, starting the engines with divers in the water, and entering/exiting the water. Additionally, because it is uncommon for these vessels to have adequate safety equipment, you should consider providing these items as part of your responsibility in planning the dive.

Seamanship and Basic Operations

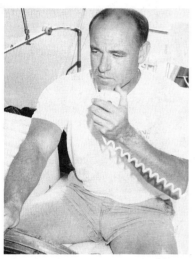

We have already mentioned that the Divemaster needs to be an adequate seaman. What, however, are the specific requirements you need to fulfill as a seaman? A general guideline to follow when you are acting as a crew member is that you should be capable of temporarily taking charge of the vessel in the event that the captain is incapacitated. Whether this will involve actually running the vessel or simply being able to properly summon assistance will depend upon the locale, the Divemaster's familiarity with boat operations and the captain's discretion.

Figure 5-12
When a Divemaster steps aboard a boat, he may become — in effect — a seaman.

Charts

While it is not necessary for the Divemaster to completely understand navigation, he should be generally familiar with navigational charts. Knowledge of these charts can aid you in selecting dive sites and will enable you to more accurately assess environmental conditions, such as bottom type and depth. Being familiar with how to determine position is also important because, in an emergency, authorities will need to know the location of the vessel as accurately as possible. Accuracy in determining that position is possible only when a compass *and* a chart are used.

Charts have varying scales. *The smaller the scale, the larger the physical areas depicted.* Coastal charts (the type used to locate most offshore dive sites) are of a smaller scale (and therefore cover more area) than a harbor chart (the type used to enter or leave a harbor). A harbor chart will, however, provide more details of the area. Always use the *largest-scale* chart possible for diving, because these charts will provide the greatest detail.

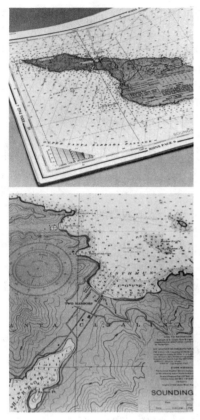

Figure 5-13a
Small-scale *charts show large areas, but little detail.*

Figure 5-13b
Large-scale *charts show small areas, but great detail.*

Nautical charts are not to be considered maps because they do not indicate what "road" or course is required for a particular destination. The course must instead be determined in relation to one's position. To determine position on a chart, you need to understand latitude and longitude. These scales will be found on the perimeters of the chart. A latitude and longitude coordinate is, by far, the most accurate determinant of position. Fixing a position relative to shore bearings can also be highly accurate, but this will require a higher degree of familiarity with the chart and an understanding of how to use a compass. It is highly advisable that you acquire these skills through additional training.

To those not familiar with them, nautical charts can appear very confusing and complicated. This is a misconception. Nautical charts appear complex because they contain a large number of symbols that indicate factors, such as depth, bottom type and navigational aids. By learning these symbols, one can more easily understand nautical charts. A complete key describing these chart symbols is contained on Na-

Figure 5-14
Nautical charts are easy to understand once the meanings of the various symbols are learned.

tional Ocean Survey Chart No. 1 and is available from many boating-supply stores. Unfortunately, few divers take full advantage of the value that nautical charts provide.

Hazards At Sea

Various devices and procedures have been established to provide safety information to those who use the waterways.

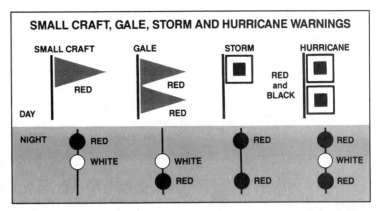

SMALL CRAFT, GALE, STORM AND HURRICANE WARNINGS

Figure 5-15
Anyone involved in boating activities
must be able to recognize signals that
indicate hazardous weather conditions.

Signals indicating small craft advisories and storm warnings are posted at all Coast Guard facilities and at most harbormaster offices. As we described in "Dive Planning," continuous weather forecasts are available over marine radio and can forewarn the Divemaster of deteriorating weather conditions.

Boaters are also notified of other hazards such as weather warnings, inoperable buoys, disabled ships or any situation that could affect the safety of a vessel by special VHF-FM marine radio announcements. These announcements are preceded by the word *Security* (pronounced *say-cur-i-tay*) spoken three times prior to the message. These transmissions are vitally important to the safety of the vessel and should be diligently monitored.

More permanent situations affecting navigational and other safety matters are published as a *Notice to Mariners*. Copies of local mariners' notices are especially useful for small-craft operators and are available free of charge by contacting the local Coast Guard District Commander.

Marine Radio Operations

A vital communications link that must be available on all charter boats is the marine (VHF-FM) radio. These radios are for messages of a *safety* or *operational* nature only (not for socializing) and are equipped with several broadcasting frequencies. The most important channel is 16. This channel is reserved for emergency communications and hailing (establishing initial contact with other stations). Once contact is properly established on channel 16, traffic must be transferred to other working channels. This procedure keeps channel 16 continually clear. Though any person may transmit a message on the VHF radio, a licensed operator must be present and responsible for the proper use of the station, except in an emergency.

Figure 5-16
The boat-based Divemaster
should have a basic understanding
of marine radio operations.

Figure 5-17
Authorities like the Coast Guard
continually monitor VHF-FM channel 16.

Particularly in an emergency, knowing how to use a marine radio is vital to the Divemaster. The Coast Guard and all other vessels not engaged in transmission must, by law, continually monitor channel 16. Therefore, in an emergency, one can be reasonably certain that a transmission on channel 16 will elicit action from authorities or other boaters. The procedure for transmitting a *life-threatening* emergency is as follows:

1. State *Mayday* three times.
2. Identify the vessel and its radio-station call letters.
3. State the vessel position (latitude and longitude or bearing from a known geographical position).
4. State the nature of the problem and the type of assistance needed.
5. Provide other information that will facilitate the rescue (complete description of the vessel, number of persons on board, etc.).

Life-threatening emergencies have the highest priority on the airway, and in this event, all other stations must cease transmission and stand by to lend assistance.

In some instances, the Coast Guard and other authorities also monitor CB (citizen's band) radio (usually channel 9). This is not a legal requirement, and is in any case a highly variable policy. When boat diving, a CB radio should never be used in lieu of a VHF marine radio.

Anchoring and Docking

One area where the Divemaster will likely become involved

Figure 5-18
During docking and anchoring
operations, the Divemaster should closely
follow the instructions of the captain.

is in anchoring and docking procedures. Both procedures are essential to the safety of the vessel and everyone on board. While the captain will be the one responsible for providing direction, you and other crew members will normally execute his directions.

Docking

The crew must know what is expected of them *well before* leaving or arriving at the dock. Leaving the dock is usually a simpler process than returning.

Once you are satisfied that everyone is aboard, you or a crew member will begin, on word from the captain, releasing the dock lines, beginning on the *leeward* side of the vessel.

Figure 5-19
When leaving the dock, the leeward *dock lines should* always *be released first.*

Releasing the lines of the windward side will cause the vessel to be blown into the dock. Before releasing the lines, always ask if the lines should come aboard the vessel or be left at the dock. Upon instructions from the captain, you should release the appropriate lines. It is important that you announce completion of this maneuver to the captain by calling out *All port lines released!* and *All starboard lines re-*

Figure 5-20
The key to safe, efficient docking is sufficient preparation and close coordination with the captain and other crew members.

leased! Once the vessel is free, the crew should stand by in case there is a need to *fend off* or clear the boat of the dock (particularly in windy weather). Vessels with only one engine are especially difficult to maneuver and may require assistance from the crew when leaving a berth.

Entering a dock can often be more difficult than leaving. The key is *preparation* and *coordination*. Well before arrival, all non-crew members should be directed away from any area likely to become busy during the docking procedure. All docking lines should be made ready and all fenders positioned outboard. As the vessel gets close to the dock, people tend to fend off using their feet or hands. This is ineffective *and* foolish because, with the exception of the smallest boats, an individual cannot oppose the force of a large vessel coming into contact with a pier or dock. If a vessel must be fended off, a fender should be in place in that position to absorb the impact and protect the hull and dock.

Knowing where and how to secure the lines is important when securing the vessel. All Divemasters and crew members must know how to properly secure a line to a mooring cleat (see Figure 5-21) — a procedure that is often done im-

Figure 5-21
An important skill for the boat-based Divemaster is knowing how to properly secure a line to a cleat.

properly. When heaving a line to someone on shore, never assume they know how to properly secure it. Always check to confirm security. Additionally, all excess line should be neatly coiled to avoid entanglement.

For safety reasons, never allow passengers to assist in docking operations. There is no way of knowing their level of competence and personal injury or damage to the vessel may result from such a mistake.

Anchoring

As in docking, all anchoring procedures should be carefully directed by the captain. All passengers should be instructed to move away from any area likely to interfere with anchoring operations. Before arriving at the site, the Divemaster or a crew member should make the anchor and rode (line) ready. As the anchor must be released quickly, be certain that it will not become entangled on deck fixtures or trip someone as it is released. The anchor rode will usually be a combination of chain and rope. The chain is used to prevent the rode from being frayed or otherwise damaged by sharp rock or coral on the bottom and also increases the anchor's holding power.

When the anchor is released, it should not be dropped directly on the dive site. The vessel's final position, due to the length of the rode, will usually be well downwind or downcurrent from the location in which the anchor was dropped. When in tropical waters, never drop an anchor directly on a reef; doing so may damage the coral. Instead, release the anchor over a sandy area between reef structures. Another even better and increasingly more common solution to the problem of reef destruction is the use of permanent mooring buoys. These buoys effectively eliminate the need to use an

Figure 5-22
As the anchor must be released quickly, the rode (line) must be made ready well in advance.

Figure 5-23
Mooring buoys make anchoring simple and easy and are an excellent means of protecting the underwater environment.

anchor, thus protecting the reef and saving the crew a great deal of physical exertion.

Once the anchor is released, the captain will provide instructions on how much *scope,* or length of line, to let out (usually at least three times the depth). The rode should be secured to a foredeck cleat or post. The anchoring operation does not, however, end here. Simply because the anchor is on the bottom does not always mean that it is holding. Before continuing with diving activities, the relative position of the vessel must be observed to determine if the anchor has dragged or is solidly holding. With practice, you can

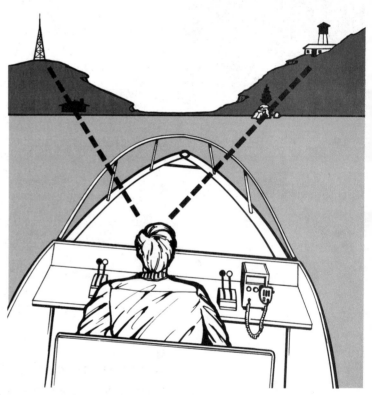

Figure 5-24
Several range bearings should be taken
and checked periodically to make certain
that the vessel is not dragging anchor.

determine the difference between a holding or dragging anchor merely by feeling the rode. Once in the water, either you or another responsible person should check the security of the anchor on the bottom. As this procedure can, occasionally, be tricky and even dangerous, it should be left to those with sufficient experience.

Unless assisted by an electric windlass, raising the anchor can be a difficult chore. This difficulty can be greatly reduced by using the proper technique. Under power, the vessel should maneuver toward the anchor's location. It is important for the person on deck to direct the captain to the

Figure 5-25
The Divemaster or another
responsible person should confirm
the security and placement of the anchor.

appropriate spot by pointing in the proper direction. As the vessel proceeds, the slack of the anchor rode may be taken aboard. As soon as the vessel is *directly above* the anchor, the captain is signaled to *stop* (engines in neutral). The remaining portion of the rode is made fast around a cleat, and the boat continues in a direction opposite the lay of the anchor. This maneuver will usually break the anchor free from the bottom, and it may be hauled aboard. (Be certain that the anchor is free of any mud before bringing it on board.) Once it is aboard, secure the anchor and stow the rode according to the captain's instructions. As this procedure could cause significant damage to a coral reef, it is important to initially anchor the vessel in a sandy area or on a mooring — as previously described — when diving on or near coral formations.

On rare occasions, the anchor may not break free due to fouling or entanglement on the bottom. In this instance, it may be necessary for a diver to return to the bottom and free the anchor by hand in order for it to be raised. Special care should be taken in this event. In particular, regardless of the inconvenience it may create, the Divemaster must avoid *solo diving* when it becomes necessary to free an anchor. Additionally, you should consider the decompression consequences of such a dive. Short, deep *bounce dives* have been shown to be especially conducive to decompression sickness.

Anchoring and docking operations are simple but will require practice to develop competence. Never attempt these procedures without prior experience, and even then, only when familiar with the vessel and requested to do so by the captain.

Suggestions for Further Training

It is far beyond the scope of the PADI Divemaster course to teach basic seamanship and boat handling, other than what has been presented here. Such skills are, however, very useful to the boat-based Divemaster. In addition to knowing how to dock and anchor the vessel, you may also find it valuable to know how to maneuver the vessel temporarily, if necessary. This knowledge is only possible through considerable experience and more specialized training. The Coast Guard and U.S. Power Squadron provide numerous courses in seamanship, navigation and safe-boating practices. The cost of this training is minimal, if not free, and is highly advised for all those responsible for supervising boat-diving activities.

Figure 5-26
Additional training on boating
and seamanship is available
from several sources. Such train-
ing is highly recommended for
the boat-based Divemaster.

Pre-Dive Procedures

While the Divemaster may not function as a crew member on every dive, he will be responsible for the supervision of divers. In general, the guidelines for supervision on board a boat are no different than those for all dives and were thoroughly discussed in "Dive Management and Control." Therefore, a review of that section is advised prior to any boat diving activity. There are other considerations relevant to diver supervision that are unique to boat diving.

Pre-Boarding and Boarding

The job of the Divemaster begins prior to the arrival of the divers. If you are acting as a crew member, you may also have various maintenance tasks to perform before taking passengers aboard. If you are diving from an unfamiliar boat, you may wish to arrive early in order to familiarize yourself with the vessel and crew.

The Divemaster's role, as always, is to ensure both the safety *and* enjoyment of those in his charge. As the divers arrive, you should welcome them aboard and make them feel

Figure 5-27
The Divemaster should welcome divers aboard in order to answer questions and establish good rapport.

comfortable. Initiating casual conversations can be useful in identifying potential problems or assigning buddy teams.

Usually all passengers will sign in on a roster as they board. It is advisable to list all non-crew members, regardless of whether they are divers or not. This information could be vital in the event of an emergency. Certification cards and log books should also be checked *before* leaving the dock, to

Figure 5-28
A good practice is to check certifica-tions and log books prior to departure.

avoid embarrassing those who may have forgotten, or do not have, proof of certification and experience.

Divers should then be instructed *how* and *where* to stow their equipment. You should check to confirm that all equip-ment is *secure.* "Landlubbers" are often not accustomed to the forces exerted by a moving boat and may not understand the difference between equipment being *put down* and be-ing *stowed.* Make certain that weight belts and other heavy objects are not prone to movement and that other items are not precariously hung over head. Tanks should be checked to confirm security and dive bags or other equipment should not be allowed to obstruct companionways, engine hatches or other critical areas. Encourage buddy teams to stow their equipment near each other to facilitate their entering the water and to keep the deck from becoming a confused, disorganized mess.

It is extremely important that the roster be *reconfirmed before* leaving the dock. Everyone on board must be on the

Figure 5-29
The dive roster should be reconfirmed *prior to departure.*

roster, and everyone on the roster must be on board. Passengers often leave the vessel once they sign in or may board without you noticing them. Unaccounted-for passengers can give rise to very frightening and embarrassing situations.

Orientation

While underway or prior to leaving the dock, thoroughly orient the passengers to the vessel and to important procedures. This orientation should emphasize safety considerations, although you should not exclude information that could make the dive more enjoyable. You must not lose sight of your goal to ensure a safe, *fun* dive for the passengers.

You should begin the orientation by explaining basic boating terminology (starboard, port, fore, aft, head, bridge, etc.). Instructions from the crew are normally communicated using proper terminology, and without a basic understanding, divers may become confused and may hinder efficiency. Having divers be familiar with terminology is also useful in the event of an emergency.

The orientation should also cover topics such as areas of the vessel that are off-limits to passengers, the location of emergency equipment (life jackets, fire extinguishers and first aid equipment), along with information on convenience

Figure 5-30
The Divemaster should conduct a formal orientation to the vessel and to boat-diving procedures.

items such as the shower, cooler and head. As marine toilets are often quite different than standard home-use models, special attention should be given to operating procedures.

It is also helpful for the Divemaster to explain what areas or provisions have been made for the storage of game and/or camera equipment. Areas set aside for cameras, in particular, should offer protection from the elements and provide ample room to do any necessary work.

Divers should be reminded to drink plenty of liquids to avoid dehydration, and to be aware of the effects of the sun. Also encourage divers to wear proper footwear in order to maintain traction on the deck. Bare feet and sandals are especially dangerous on wet decks.

On-Deck Rules

There are several *on-deck* rules that are useful in maintaining safety and efficiency while on board. These usually include the following:

1. Assembly of the regulator/BCD and other appropriate equipment should take place when possible *before leaving the dock.* (But keep the equipment out of the way.) It

Figure 5-31
Preparing equipment prior to departure can often save time and inconvenience.

is far more difficult to complete these operations while underway; waiting until the boat arrives at the dive site may cause a needless delay.

2. *Always* use a dive bag or similar container when boat diving. It will prevent equipment loss, and working out of a bag helps to prevent equipment cluttering up an already-sparse deck area. You may need to tactfully remind divers about the stowage of gear in bags.

3. Because the working area on the vessel is often limited and not very stable, several rules should be observed relative to equipment. Divers should never be allowed to walk on deck while wearing fins; fins should be donned only as divers are preparing to enter the water. Additionally,

Figure 5-32
The Divemaster should never allow divers wearing fins to walk on deck.

Figure 5-33
Donning tanks overhead is an unsafe
practice — particularly when boat diving.

never allow tanks to be donned over the head, as the risk of falling or injuring others is too great.

In addition to those stated, dive boats often have their own distinctive rules and procedures. You should always check with the captain or crew members to determine and to abide by these unique rules.

Emergency Procedures

It is essential that divers understand what they should do in the event of an emergency. These procedures may vary with the circumstances. Most often, the Divemaster establishes a recall procedure that gets divers back on board in a timely and efficient manner. Usually, diver recall is done while the

Figure 5-34
Because an emergency will require
close coordination of activities,
supervisory personnel should have a
preestablished plan of action.

vessel is still at anchor, although some captains may prefer to pick divers up while the vessel is under power.

In some life-threatening emergencies requiring quick action, the captain may elect to have the vessel leave the dive site without recalling all divers. This is done only if another vessel is within the immediate area and can quickly recover those still in the water. Whatever procedure is used, it must be clearly communicated to the divers to prevent confusion and injury.

Entry Considerations

Even when the boat is anchored, divers should never enter the water until the Divemaster instructs them to do so. Some-

times the anchor must be reset, which requires that the boat be under power. This is a very dangerous maneuver if divers are already in the water — especially if the crew is unaware of their presence.

Divers should be instructed to enter the water only at the designated entry areas, using the safest, easiest techniques. Prior to divers entering the water, you may conduct a quick pre-dive safety check as described in "Dive Management and Control." Once a diver has entered the water, he should give you the *OK* signal and swim away from the immediate area while awaiting his buddy. Divers should never descend until both buddies are in the water and prepared to descend *together.*

Figure 5-35
Divers should be allowed to enter the water only at designated entry points.

In-Water Procedures

Most of the in-water procedures unique to boat diving involve maintaining orientation and proximity to the vessel. Divers should attempt to stay in front of the vessel at all times so that upon surfacing they may use any existing current to assist them when swimming back to the boat. Remaining in front of the boat may be accomplished by taking a compass bearing in the direction from which the current is flowing and maintaining a position relative to this course throughout the dive. Another useful technique when diving in shallow water is to have the diver ascend to the surface when he depletes approximately half his air supply, note the position of the boat and continue the dive in the direction of the vessel. As a safety measure, instruct divers to come back *on board the vessel* with 300-500 psi of air in their tanks.

Figure 5-36
Require divers to signal OK anytime they surface.

To assist divers who mistakenly get far behind the boat and cannot swim against the current, it is advisable to use a *stern line.* A stern line consists of a 100- to 300-foot/30 to 90 metre (depending upon conditions) floating polypropylene line trailed behind the boat with a highly visible float at the end. Divers caught behind the vessel can simply swim to the line and pull themselves, or can be hauled back to the boat instead of having to attempt swimming against the current.

As the vast majority of problems occur *on the surface,* a trained, alert individual must remain on board at all times to supervise the dive site. Ideally this *lookout* should *not* be the boat captain, because he will need to devote full attention to operating the vessel in an emergency.

The lookout should be *attentively* positioned at the highest point on the vessel with a pair of binoculars to facilitate observation. Highly experienced individuals are able to keep track of divers while they are under water on relatively calm days by watching for bubble trails. Particular attention should be paid to any divers observed *behind* the vessel. The lookout should always be diligent and prepared to respond *immediately* (or to direct the response) to anyone who may require assistance.

All divers should be instructed to give the *OK* signal to the boat, and this signal should be confirmed and returned by the lookout. Divers who do not demonstrate the *OK* signal should be assumed to have a problem, and preparation for assistance should be initiated. Rarely will divers who are truly experiencing problems remember to give the proper *distress* signal.

If assistance becomes necessary, the rescuer must be properly equipped before he enters the water. He should therefore have a mask, fins, snorkel, adequate exposure protection and a flotation device that can be extended to the victim available at all times. As we mentioned previously, a rescue board (or better still, a "chase boat") is also extremely useful for quick in-water response.

Figure 5-37
An effective Divemaster must be well-prepared and vigilant.

Exiting and Post-Dive Procedures

Exiting the water must be done smoothly and properly to avoid injury. Using an improper technique may cause divers to be injured by the roll and pitch of the boat, or they may accidentally fall upon others still in the water.

Any boat that is considered adequate for diving will have some form of ladder, platform or similar device that will enable divers to board the vessel. To avoid severely injuring

Figure 5-38
Caution divers remaining in the water to not get too close to those exiting.

Figure 5-39
The Divemaster should know how to properly handle expensive camera systems and other equipment items.

themselves, divers should be warned to stay out from under the exit device. Only one diver at a time should be allowed on the ladder, with no one immediately behind that individual (in case the diver falls backward). Instruct the diver to keep his mask and regulator or snorkel in place during the exit. Circumstance and personal preference will dictate when and where fins are removed. If a diver prefers to remove his fins prior to climbing the ladder, he should remove them only after he has secured a firm position on the ladder. Some divers prefer, however, to wear their fins throughout the exiting process. This procedure may be permissible if the divers are capable and the ladder permits such an exit.

Because divers will probably be tired, they may enter the boat in a manner that may subject it to unexpected rocking. You must be prepared to lend assistance at a moment's notice. Be aware that divers will be especially concerned about the safety of their camera systems. Normally, cameras (and other unsecured equipment) are handed up to the Divemaster prior to the exit. You must know how to properly handle this equipment to avoid damaging it and possibly injuring other divers.

Once divers are aboard, you should ascertain dive-profile information from each diver, including the *maximum depth* and *bottom time.* An important exception to this procedure may involve those divers using computerized decompression devices; we will discuss this further in the section "Deep Diving Supervision: Theory and Practice." Additionally, divers should be instructed to move away from the immediate exit area and to take any personal equipment with them. Fins, in particular, are often left in the path of exiting divers and can cause falls. Excessive cluttering of the decks with equipment can also be avoided if divers are encouraged to pack their equipment into dive bags as soon as possible.

Once all divers are back aboard, you should call roll and *visually* confirm that *everyone* is on board. Allowing one diver to answer for another is not a wise practice because it can easily result in confusion. After roll call, divers should be encouraged to log their dives, and you should remain available to sign the log entries.

Only after the last dive of the day should divers be allowed to drink alcohol, and even then, encourage moderation. The affects of alcohol on the development of decompression sickness are unknown, but indications are that drinking soon after diving may predispose the diver to bends.

Figure 5-40
The dive roster should be confirmed
visually prior *to departing the dive site.*

Figure 5-41
Being able to deal with seasickness
is an inevitable part of being a
boat-based Divemaster.

Avoiding Seasickness

Although the subject of avoiding seasickness may not be vital to proper supervisory technique, it is a common concern among boat divers. As the Divemaster will often have to deal with seasickness or its effects, it is necessary to be somewhat familiar with the subject.

It is thought that seasickness involves the vestibular apparatus of the inner ear and that visual/perceptual disorientation is a significant factor in causing the disorder. Based partially on fact and common experience, the following advice may be helpful in avoiding seasickness. You should make the divers aware of this information when appropriate.

1. Divers should avoid eating greasy foods prior to boarding and while aboard the boat.

2. If seasickness medication is to be taken, advise divers to always know its effects before using it prior to diving. Be aware that due to significant side effects, transdermal medications (usually applied via a patch behind the ear) are *not* recommended prior to diving.

3. If the decision is made to take a known, acceptable medication for seasickness, divers should be advised to always do so *well prior* to departure (often the night before diving). Most medication is ineffective if taken when seasick.

4. While underway, divers prone to seasickness should be advised to remain on deck and not to go below unless necessary.

5. As visual orientation is thought to be very important in avoiding seasickness, divers should be advised to maintain

Figure 5-42
Seasickness medication should
always be taken well before it is needed.

Figure 5-43
Divers experiencing symptoms of
seasickness should be advised to remain
on deck and to get plenty of fresh air.

eye contact with the horizon or other stationary, land-based object.

6. All divers should be advised to stay away from areas near to exhaust fumes (transom, engine room, etc.).

7. Seasickness-prone divers should be advised to try to stay busy while underway, but should *not* read.

8. Finally, advise seasick-prone divers to always be prepared to enter the water as soon as possible. Most individuals become seasick not while underway, but after the vessel is at anchor. The less time spent on board, the less likely that seasickness will occur.

Figure 5-44
Divers prone to seasickness should plan
to enter the water as soon as possible.

Finally, if it should become necessary for a diver to vomit, have him do so over the *leeward* rail. Divers should never use the head for this purpose. Should the vomiting become persistent, have the diver rest in a cool, shaded area and drink fluids to avoid dehydration.

Summary

In this section, we discussed how to *supervise* boat dives, which is distinctly different from general boat-diving procedures. The first portion of this section dealt with the types of vessels used for diving and the various safety and legal considerations.

We examined the Divemaster's *role as a seaman* and detailed information related to understanding nautical charts, to hazards at sea, and to marine-radio operations; with the major emphasis being on the Divemaster's role in docking and anchoring procedures. A recommendation was

Figure 5-45
Seamanship is a vital part of being an effective boat-based Divemaster.

also offered on where to find additional training in seamanship.

We also discussed the actual pre-diving and diving procedures related to boat-diving supervision. The pre-diving supervisory procedures discussed were pre-boarding and boarding, orientation, on-deck rules, emergency procedures and entry considerations. Finally, in-water, exiting and post-dive procedures were outlined in addition to information on how to avoid seasickness.

The most important lesson to be learned from this section is, when supervising a boat dive, the Divemaster must be concerned with far more than the usual duties of diver supervision. When you step aboard a boat in such a responsible role, you may be required to act as a crew member. Even if not acting as a crew member, you will often have to make decisions based upon your understanding of sound seamanship and apparent nondiving considerations. You may easily conclude from the information in this section that supervising boat diving requires a wider range of knowledge and experience than any other activity in which the Divemaster is likely to function.

Name _____

Date _____

Knowledge Review
Boat Diving Supervision and Control

1. What factors determine the type of boat used for diving in a particular location?

_____

_____

_____

_____

2. What are the legal requirements for both the vessel and its captain concerning the operation of a dive-charter boat?

_____

_____

_____

_____

3. Other than what is legally required, what are some of the general safety requirements/features of a boat used for diving activities?

_____

_____

_____

_____

4. In terms of seamanship, what is the general guideline for a Divemaster who is acting as a crew member?

_____

_____

_____

_____

5. Why is it so helpful to the boat-based Divemaster to be familiar with nautical charts?

_____

_____

_____

_____

6. By what means can a Divemaster determine potentially hazardous sea conditions?

_____

_____

_____

_____

7. What type of radio should be used for communications on board a boat? What purposes is this radio to be used for?

_____

_____

_____

_____

8. Explain what function a Divemaster who is acting as a crew member on board a dive boat may be expected to perform regarding the *docking* of the vessel.

_____

_____

_____

_____

9. When acting as a crew member on board a dive boat, what are the Divemaster's primary considerations regarding how the vessel is to be anchored?

_____

_____

_____

_____

10. Explain what pre-dive procedures the Divemaster should perform relative to boat-diving activities.

_____

_____

_____

_____

11. What instructions should the Divemaster give divers to help them avoid problems while diving from a boat?

_____

_____

_____

_____

12. What techniques are useful in helping the Divemaster maintain supervision of the dive site from a boat?

_____

_____

_____

_____

13. What are the most important considerations in the exit/post-dive phase of a boat dive?

_____

_____

_____

_____

14. What are some techniques useful in avoiding seasickness?

_____

_____

_____

_____

Six

Deep Diving Supervision: Theory and Practice

Section Objectives

☐ List and explain the function of specialized equipment necessary for safe participation in deep-diving activities.

☐ Explain the procedure for diver and environmental assessments suggested for use in deep-diving activities.

☐ Describe the techniques and procedures by which deep-diving activities may be organized to obtain maximum control and safety.

☐ Explain why the Recreational Dive Planner was developed, and what advantages it provides over other tables.

☐ Explain how the Recreational Dive Planner was developed and tested.

☐ Explain why there are two versions of the Recreational Dive Planner, and what advantage The Wheel has over the Table.

☐ Use the required special rules for the Recreational Dive Planner including: Multiple Repetitive

Dives; Safety Stops; Emergency Decompression; Omitted Decompression; Diving at Altitude; and Flying After Diving.

☐ **Explain the basic concept and operation of a dive computer and how to encourage proper use of these devices.**

Introduction

This section details important concepts and proper procedures for the organization of deep-diving activities. The significant physiological problems that may result from breathing high-pressure air at depth, the inability to quickly reach the surface in an emergency, and the typical diver's

Figure 6-1
Deep diving presents unique problems both to its participants and to those who supervise them.

lack of training and experience in this area combine to make deep diving one of the most potentially hazardous underwater activities. This is not to say, however, that deep diving should not be practiced; only that it requires special attention and professional supervision. When you supervise and control deep-diving activities, they require your utmost awareness and planning.

The approach of this section will also differ from previous sections of this manual. While the first portion will consider specific procedures relating to the supervision of deep diving, the second portion will address important theoretical concepts necessary for a thorough understanding of the dive tables. It is hoped that this section will clearly demonstrate how supervisory personnel can maximize the safety of deep diving through proper planning and awareness of common

Figure 6-2
As deep diving is potentially one of the most hazardous forms of diving, proper supervision requires careful planning and consideration.

problems. Before proceeding in this section, it is advised that you review the segment on "Deep Diving" within section Five of *The Encyclopedia of Recreational Diving.*

Although *deep* may be considered a relative term, deep diving is usually considered to be any dive made in excess of 60 feet. However, the prudent Divemaster must understand that in many instances dives to even shallower depths may be ill-advised for some divers, depending upon individual experience. While the upward limit of deep diving may be interpretive, the maximum end of the scale is absolute. *Under no circumstances should recreational diving activities take place below a depth of 130 feet/40 metres.*

Equipment

The Divemaster's personal diving equipment needs differ little from any other deep diver. You should, however, give consideration to the fact that you may be required to remain in the water longer than other divers, and may need to lend assistance to others. Obviously, only top-quality equipment will meet such rigorous demands. Specific personal items essential for the supervision and control of deep diving include an adequate air supply and exposure protection, a high-quality regulator and alternate air source, and accurate depth and timing devices.

The adequacy of the air supply will be dependent upon the depth of the dive, your air consumption rate and environmental factors, such as temperature and current. Exposure protection will also depend upon variable environment factors and your susceptibility to cold. While it is difficult to provide a hard and fast rule concerning air supply and exposure protection, a general guideline for you should be "provide for more warmth and air than you think you will need."

As depth places increased demands upon regulator performance, only a balanced or similarly designed regulator should be considered for supervisory personnel such as the Divemaster. Alternate-air-source devices — whether "octopus" units or totally redundant systems — must be maintained in top working order. For additional insight into the use of alternate-air-source devices, it is advisable to review pages 78-79 of the PADI *Rescue Diver Manual.*

An accurate track of bottom time and depth is essential to avoid decompression-related problems, and a high-quality watch or timing device plus a depth gauge are required for all supervisory personnel (and highly recommended for all other divers). Special consideration should also be given to

Figure 6-3
The equipment needed for deep diving is often more extensive and sophisticated.

Figure 6-4
Computerized decompression devices are becoming increasingly common for deep-diving application.

the accuracy of the instruments. Depth gauges are designed to be accurate to within one or two feet, *if they are calibrated.* Because of the importance of the depth gauge, you should have your gauge tested and recalibrated at least annually. When faced with inconsistent readings from more than one gauge while under water, the safest practice is to *assume the deepest reading gauge is the correct one.*

Other devices recently introduced to the diving market can have a great impact on the ease and safety of deep diving. These devices are the recently developed dive computers. While the basic theoretical model for these devices will be discussed later in this section, there are several considerations relating to their use that are appropriate for discussion here. If it is likely that you will be supervising divers who use these devices, you should be familiar with the operating instructions and guidelines for each device. Divers should be required to adhere strictly to the manufacturer's guidelines and under no circumstance should they alter the device or deviate from the instructions for its use.

When you are supervising divers using dive computers, stress that each diver in the buddy team must have his own device. Do not allow sharing of a single computer among two divers because the team will not dive the *exact* same profile. Also, use the more conservative computer to plan the progress of the dive and subsequent repetitive dives. Advise owner of computers to clearly mark each device to avoid confusion when the devices are removed during surface intervals. Finally, warn divers never to turn off their computers if they plan to make a repetitive dive.

Equipment required for supervising dives can be classified into two categories: 1) safety and 2) communication/information. Safety equipment may include spare tanks to set up the *safety stop* (detailed later) and down lines to enable divers to maintain orientation while under water. Communication and information equipment includes the Recreational Dive Planners and Data Carrier, PADI Aquatic Cue Cards (Open Water), Divemaster Slates and a large blank underwater slate. A means of easily identifying divers while under water is also helpful when in large groups.

Dive-Site Selection

Special care must be exercised in the selection of an appropriate dive site because of the problems associated with deep diving. The Divemaster or other supervisory personnel

Figure 6-5
Favorable environmental conditions and
close supervision are important
considerations for a safe deep dive.

should be thoroughly familiar with the area and have previous experience in the conditions presented.

Other environmental factors like current and visibility are especially important in selecting a deep-dive location. Unless the dive is to be specifically organized as a drift dive, deep diving in strong currents should be avoided. The energy expenditure required to fight a current, combined with the increased breathing resistance and air-consumption rate brought about by the deeper environment, can easily result in a potentially hazardous situation. Deep diving while visibility is poor is contradictory to safe deep-diving practices. Adequate supervision is difficult in low visibility, and such conditions also increase the anxiety level (and probably the air-consumption rate) of the divers.

Cold temperatures may have an unsuspected effect on dive supervision. Deep water is generally colder than the surface, and the difference in temperatures may be extreme. Divers should be instructed to wear more exposure protection than normal. Cold temperatures may also affect the divers' mental state while under water.

Diver Assessment

Prior deep-diving experience is highly advised because the potential danger can be greater than with most other forms of diving. Those making a deep dive for the first time should ideally be under the supervision of a qualified instructor. Whereas your function usually is to supervise those who already possess an acceptable degree of experience, this is not always feasible. If you do supervise an individual's first deep-diving

Figure 6-6
When accompanying deep divers,
the Divemaster should remain alert
for any abnormal behavior or
signs of impaired judgment.

experience, very close in-water supervision is advised.

When supervising deep dives be aware that divers often need help with using dive tables. This is to be expected. Most dives are made within shallow ranges where ample bottom time exists. This is not the case when deep diving. Once certified, divers will often leave issues such as maximum bottom time, surface interval and other table-related matters up to

Figure 6-7
A brief discussion prior to the
dive can often provide insight
into the diver's mental state.

those who are supervising them. Although not advised, this is only human.

The most important aspect to doing an effective job is the attitude you convey to the divers. Make it known that you are available for consultation should questions concerning tables use arise. Secondly, if you are asked for assistance, don't act as though the diver experiencing the problem is incompetent or that such questions are an imposition. Gladly answer the question, pointing out how the error was made. You must avoid conveying an attitude that may discourage questions concerning the use of the tables. The consequence of tables ignorance is far too great.

Unquestionably, the most common problem concerning the use of the dive tables involves repetitive diving. Most often divers forget to add their residual nitrogen time (RNT) to their actual bottom time (ABT) in order to arrive at the total bottom time (TBT) of the dive. There is a simple and very effective memory device to avoid this all-too-common problem. Instruct divers to "Always remember to drown the RAT between dives." This colorful phrase helps assure that they will remember to add the residual nitrogen time (R) to the actual bottom time (A) to determine the total bottom time (T), or R + A = T. Another way of avoiding this problem is to encourage use of The Wheel. Due to its design, the user never has to account for confusing and theoretical concepts such as "residual nitrogen time," and distinguishing actual from total bottom time.

The other common error is simply forgetting how to work through the tables. Fortunately, many tools exist to help divers overcome problems related to using the dive tables. Using the Recreational Dive Planner, in particular, greatly reduces this problem. The Table's continuous-flow format make it very simple to use. The Wheel, once learned, is even easier. Another tool at your disposal to prevent errors regarding table use is the Data Carrier, which comes as part of every Wheel package. On one side it contains a useful "memory jogger" on how use The Wheel. The other side has space to compute a single, repetitive and multilevel dive. There's even space for a contingency plan in case you alter your planned profile. All divers, especially when diving deep, should be encouraged to have and use this valuable device.

Other useful tools for you are the giant-sized versions of the Recreational Dive Planner. These tables are not only oversized (making them easy to use with large groups), but they are also completely waterproof. Keep in mind, however, that the Wheel version is *not calibrated.* While its a useful tool for showing divers how to The Wheel. It should never be used to plan an actual open-water dive. Always use a standard-size, calibrated Wheel for actual dive planning purposes.

Another factor relative to diver assessment is the motive for the dive. Occasionally, divers are tempted to dive for no

Figure 6-8
After exiting the water,
divers should be observed for
signs of decompression sickness.

reason other than "going deep." This practice should be strongly discouraged because it accomplishes nothing and can result in divers being exposed to needless risk. Divers seeking extensive training in deep diving should be encouraged to enroll in a PADI Deep Diver specialty course.

The observant Divemaster should also be alert for the anxiety that a deep dive may create both above *and* below the water. As with night diving, deep diving may be more psychologically demanding than other forms of diving. You must therefore provide a means for the diver to call off a dive without fear of ridicule or peer pressure. Obviously, any individual who begins a deep dive in a high state of anxiety bears special attention; deep-diving conditions could easily aggravate an already less-than-ideal situation.

Due to the increased physical demands placed on the diver in the deep environment like greater heat loss and breathing exertion, deep divers should be encouraged to eat properly and get sufficient rest prior to the dive. High-energy, easily digestible foods such as a candy bar or dried fruits and nuts are good foods to eat prior to diving. As always, dehydration should also be avoided by drinking plenty of non-carbonated, nonalcoholic fluids. Good common sense suggests a proper diet is important in avoiding decompression sickness and in avoiding other physiological problems associated with diving.

There is one final aspect of diver assessment that most Divemasters tend to overlook. This aspect involves *post*-dive activities. Because of the nature of decompression sickness, divers are rarely affected immediately upon exit. Typically, the initial signs of decompression sickness appear 30 minutes to several hours after the dive. To reduce the risk of decompression sickness, divers should be encouraged to avoid taking hot showers and any form of strenuous physical activity immediately after a deep dive. Excessive alcohol intake should also be avoided after deep diving so that symptoms of any potential decompression sickness will not be masked. Most importantly, you should remember that when in doubt about a possible dive-related symptom, you should not hesitate to seek advice from a knowledgeable diving physician or the Divers Alert Network (DAN).*

*Contact and membership information for DAN is contained in the Appendix.

Supervision Procedures

While many forms of diving are more easily supervised from the surface, this is usually *not* the case in deep diving. Adequate in-water supervision is advised at all times. If the group is too large for a single Divemaster to supervise, and no other trained supervisory personnel are available, consider, at the least, assigning an experienced deep diver to each dive team.

Figure 6-9
A contingency plan will enable the Divemaster to act quickly in the event of some unforeseen incident.

Figure 6-10
Regardless of their experience level, all divers are affected to varying degrees by nitrogen at depth.

Contingency Planning

Rarely is a dive made at a uniform depth. Additionally, the actual depth of a dive may be different than planned. To provide for any unexpected change in the dive plan, the Divemaster should have a *contingency plan* that seeks to answer the question *What if?* What if the dive is deeper or shallower than planned? What if the planned bottom time is exceeded? What if emergency decompression is required? All of these questions are crucial to the interest of safety, and you must be prepared to respond.

In-Water Techniques

In-water supervision must take two vital factors into consideration: 1) the considerable increase in the density of the air will cause divers to expend more air and more energy than normal; and 2) the narcotic effects of increased partial pressures of nitrogen will make the divers less aware of themselves and their surroundings than normal. The Divemaster must therefore *be prepared to use* an alternate-air-source device should the need arise. You must remain continually alert for divers who display behavior that could be the result of nitrogen-narcosis impairment. Inattentiveness, decreased responsiveness and irrational behavior are especially indicative of nitrogen narcosis.

While under water, you should stress the need for the group to remain in close proximity. This is particularly important during the descent. You must exercise care to assure everyone descends in a safe, controlled manner. Especially if the descent is initiated in *blue water* (water in which you are unable to see the bottom), you must be able to compensate for the effects of any current. The use of a down line has several advantages in this instance; it provides a means for divers to orient themselves, and it provides an easy means for you to control the descent rate.

Upon reaching the bottom, you should continually monitor the divers' air supplies, assure that divers remain with the group and prevent divers from exceeding the prescribed maximum depth. The ascent is to be initiated as soon as the first diver reaches the predetermined minimum air supply.

Figure 6-11
To reduce both the risk of decompression sickness and lung over expansion injury, encourage divers to take a safety stop at the conslusion of every dive.

Figure 6-12
Buoyancy-control skills become especially critical when diving on underwater walls.

Figure 6-13
When supervising wall dives, the Divemaster often remains below the group to control the depth of the dive.

You should establish a *turnaround point* (usually not less than 500 psi) during the dive briefing.

To decrease the risk of decompression sickness, divers should be advised to take a "safety stop" prior to surfacing from a deep dive. Precise guidelines for when and how to make such a stop will be detailed in a later section. While safety stops are encouraged, recreational divers should never engage in planned decompression diving involving "required" decompression stops.

To facilitate the safety stop, you may wish to have divers ascend using the weighted down line to maintain proximity to the exit, more easily maintain the desired depth and reduce the effects of wave action. The down line is particularly useful because, due to the positive buoyancy produced by a near-empty tank, remaining at a constant depth can be difficult without assistance. Additional weights and tanks may also be secured to the down line at the intended depth of the safety stop to ensure that divers have sufficient air and buoyancy aids to complete the procedure.

While safety stops are becoming standard practice in deep diving, knowing what to do with the additional bottom time resulting from the stop is not as prevalent.

Finally, you may wish to incorporate an added degree of conservatism by *adding the safety stop time to the bottom time of the dive.* While this practice is not required according to the rules of use for the Recreational Dive Planner, it is advisable when deep diving.

Diving on Walls and Dropoffs

Some of the most outstanding diving is done in areas where relatively shallow bottom makes an abrupt vertical drop to abysmal depths. Such dive sites are often referred to as *walls*. While providing exceptional diving, wall dives present unique supervision problems of which you must be aware.

Because these sites are usually near open ocean, wall diving is typically accompanied by excellent visibility. In fact, visibility can be so great that divers can easily lose track of depth, only to find themselves in extreme depths very quickly. Divers are often inclined to go "just a little deeper," because it may be difficult to believe that such warm, clear water could be dangerous. Unfortunately, the same narcotic effect of nitrogen will occur at depth regardless of the clarity of the water.

To avoid problems resulting from this unique and often hypnotic form of diving, you have two courses of action. One is to require that the group dive in very close proximity to you acting as the group leader. When using this technique the depth at which you remain is the maximum limit, and no one should descend beyond this point. The other approach for you is to exercise less direct control of the entire group and assume a position near the wall to prevent others from descending deeper than the predetermined maximum depth. Remaining *behind* the group also provides a better vantage point from which to observe divers, because stragglers are more easily detected. During the briefing, you should caution the group about the unique concerns in this form of diving and stress the need for a high degree of awareness and good buoyancy-control techniques. Regardless of which approach is taken, under no circumstance should divers be allowed to go below the predetermined depth limit you established. Additionally, when supervising a deep dive, you normally should be the first one in the water so that you may be in a position to recognize and respond to descent-related problems.

Understanding Dive Tables

As a PADI diving professional your knowledge about the background and use of dive tables must be beyond a basic level. You will be responsible for decisions concerning dive profiles, surface intervals and other factors that help divers avoid decompression sickness. In addition, divers will often ask you questions concerning table use. In short, divers will look to you as an expert.

Your job is further complicated by the changing technology of our times. Years ago as there was only one standard for planning the decompression status of a dive — the U.S. Navy Tables. Therefore, questions concerning decompression were easily answered. Today its not so easy.

As a Divemaster you will be supervising divers using various means of determining their decompression status. In terms of tables, while the Recreational Dive Planner distributed by PADI is now the PADI Standard for recreational diving, you will still be confronted by divers using the U.S. Navy Tables. You may even see tables other than the RDP or U.S. Navy.

You must also consider the increasing popularity of dive computers. Today there are about two dozen different models on the market. These devices magnify the complexity of your job because of their ability to calculate a diver's decompression status based on his precise dive profile. Fur-

Figure 6-14
The Divemaster should encourage questions from divers who are unclear on how to use the dive tables.

thermore, even the decompression model programmed into the computer's memory is not standard. In fact, there are currently at least three different decompression models in use, and each manufacture often incorporates some form of refinement to whatever basic model is used. As a result, the issue of how to supervise divers using "multiple standards" — both tables and computers — is one of the most significant dilemmas facing diving professionals today. This points up the need for you to have a thorough knowledge of decompression theory and dive table design.

Figure 6-15
Supervising divers can be complicated by the fact that there are so many different types of tables and computers available today.

Before continuing in this section, you should expand your knowledge of decompression and hyperbaric physiology. An excellent way to do this is by reading page 2-17 through 2-30 of *The Encyclopedia of Recreational Diving.* A review of that material will further your understanding of the following section. For even more insight into the issues discussed in this section it is also suggested that you read the PADI publication *The Recreational Diver's Guide to Decompression Theory, Dive Tables and Computers.*

Figure 6-16
The Divemaster must be extremely competent in using the dive tables so that he may respond to frequent questions.

Early Models of Decompression

In the early twentieth century a Scottish physiologist by the name of John Scott Haldane set up the basic theoretical concept used for most dive tables and computers used today. Haldane was commissioned by the British Royal Navy to improve their crude methods of decompression and to enable dives to more extended depths. To this end Haldane reasoned that a diver, on ascent, could withstand a certain degree of overpressurization in his tissues without the formation of nitrogen bubbles. The problem was determining

$$\frac{\triangle P}{\triangle t} = (P_1 - P)\,\frac{s_1 V}{s_2 V}$$

Figure 6-17
The original conceptual model for many of the dive tables currently in use was established by the English physiologist, J.S. Haldane, near the turn of the century.

exactly how much overpressurization a diver could tolerate. Based on experiments with goats, Haldane determined this critical ratio to be 1.58. This meant the tissues of the body could tolerate 1.58 times more nitrogen pressure than the ambient pressure reached on ascent without causing decompression sickness. To exceed the critical ratio, he believed, would result in the bends.

The complete answer to the problem of decompression sickness was not as straightforward as determining a simple ratio. Several factors related to the function and makeup of the human body complicated matters. Specifically, Haldane realized that the rate of nitrogen uptake and elimination was not constant for all parts of the body. The rate varied because the amount of blood flow (referred to as perfusion) varies throughout the body.

Additionally, Haldane recognized that the various tissues of the body — blood, fat, muscle, bone — have different densities. Therefore, the speed at which gas disperses throughout the cells of a tissue (referred to as diffusion) will vary according to the type of tissue in question. These varying rates of perfusion and diffusion made the development of a decompression model quite a challenge.

Haldane solved the problem of variable rates of gas exchange by dividing the body into five theoretical "tissue compartments." The compartments, he presumed, represented all of the various possible tissue absorption and elimination rates within the body. This was the beginning of what has been termed the multi-tissue model of decompression.

Next, Haldane built a mathematical model. This model determined the amount of time it took to absorb half the amount of nitrogen required to saturate the tissue compartment. He believed desaturation would occur at the same rate. This was the origin of the tissue half-time concept. In six half-times a compartment was considered to be either full or empty. For example, Haldane selected five minutes as his fastest compartment. This compartment takes 30 minutes (six times five) to reach saturation. Similarly, his slowest tissue compartment was 75 minutes. Therefore, in seven and a half hours (six time 75 minutes), saturation occurs.

TISSUE HALF-TIMES

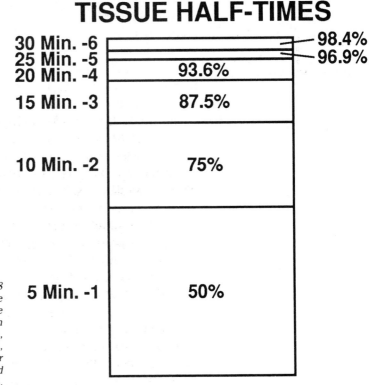

30 Min. -6 — 98.4%
25 Min. -5 — 96.9%
20 Min. -4 — 93.6%
15 Min. -3 — 87.5%
10 Min. -2 — 75%
5 Min. -1 — 50%

Figure 6-18
This illustration represents a five-minute tissue compartment. In the first five minutes it fills to 50% of its maximum pressure. In 10 minutes it is 75%, 15 minutes 87.5%, 20 minutes 93.6%, 25 minutes 96.9%. And finally after 30 minutes it is considered to be full at 98.4%.

By being able to calculate nitrogen pressure within any compartment, Haldane was able to determine the time and depth from which a diver could ascend without exceeding the maximum allowable nitrogen pressure in any one compartment. If the diver exceeded the maximum tissue pressure, then a decompression stop was required. Halting the ascent at predetermined intervals allowed for reduction in the nitrogen pressure within the diver's tissues. Once the stop was completed, the tissue pressures were reduced and the diver could then ascend to the surface.

Haldane knew that each compartment absorbed and eliminated nitrogen at differing rates. Therefore, his model provided for the compartment that came closest to the maximum allowable pressure to exercise "control" over the decompression requirement. Because of the varying rates of absorption/elimination, this control shifts among the different compartments throughout the dive according to the diver's depth and time. Considering the limits of his technology, Haldane's concepts represented a giant leap in both the theory and practice of decompression physiology.

The next important development occurred in the mid-1950's. At that time the U.S. Navy began a project to revise their existing decompression tables. Building upon Haldane's work, they made two important changes. First, the Navy found that to improve the safety and reliability of their decompression schedules it was necessary to consider more and slower tissue compartments in their model than Haldane did. The compartments they selected were: 5, 10, 20, 40, 80 and 120 minutes. (Today some models consider tissue compartments even slower than 120 minutes).

Secondly, the Navy found that Haldane's critical ratio of 1: 58 did not hold for all compartments. While Haldane's ratio worked for slower compartments, a greater ratio was allowable for faster ones. The discovery of different ratios for different tissues was the basis for what the Navy termed M values. The M value is the maximum allowable nitrogen pressure that can be tolerated by each particular compartment during pressure reduction (surfacing). Exceeding the limit in any compartment is likely to result in an increased possibility of decompression sickness.

This theoretical model was tested against actual manned dives to allow further revision and refinement. Based on this development and testing, the "U.S. Navy Standard Air Decompression Tables" were published in the late 1950's. These tables served as the standard for avoiding decompression sickness in scuba divers up until the introduction of the

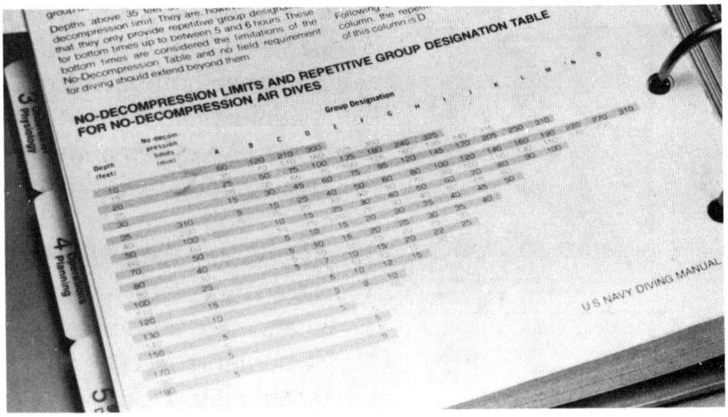

Figure 6-19
Up until the development of the Recreational Dive Planner, the U.S. Navy Standard Air Decompression Tables were the basis for most sport diving.

Recreational Dive Planner in 1988.

Since the U.S. Navy Tables were the standard for recreational diving, all the various "dive tables" published within the recreational diving community were merely a reconfiguration of these tables. This was true even for the old PADI Dive Tables, which were introduced in 1978. These, too, were actually the U.S. Navy tables condensed in size and reformatted for ease of use.

Figure 6-20
The U.S. Navy Tables were developed primarily for decompression diving and limited repetitive diving. They were never intended for the extended repetitive diving which is commonplace for sport divers.

The Development of the Recreational Dive Planner

The original intent of both Haldane's and the U.S. Navy tables were to permit reasonably safe decompression diving. But recreational divers should avoid the need for decompression completely. So, while the U.S. Navy tables served scuba

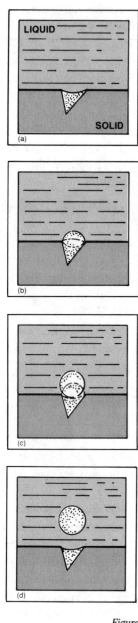

Figure 6-21
According to one current theory,
microscopic gas pockets exist in the walls
of body tissues (a) during ascent, nitrogen
dissolves from the blood and other tissues
into these pockets (b) when enough
nitrogen dissolves into the pocket, a
bubble breaks away (c) the microscopic,
loose bubble (d) eventually travels
through the bloodstream to the lungs,
where it is eliminated.

divers well for many years, they were not primarily designed for the type of diving done by recreational divers, i.e. repetitive, no-decompression diving.

A further example of how the U.S. Navy Tables were not designed for recreational diving involves repetitive diving. Making numerous repetitive dives is commonplace for scuba divers. During an extended vacation, for example, a recreational diver might make fifteen or more dives in only five or six days. The U.S. Navy Tables were never intended for such use. In fact, they were only tested for a single repetitive dive, and for not more than a single day! This misapplication might help explain in part some cases of decompression sickness following dives that are apparently "within the tables."

With the growth of recreational diving, and increased recognition of the Navy Tables' shortcomings, the time had come for change. Many believed that a new "custom tailored" set of tables should be designed for recreational diving applications (no-decompression, repetitive dives to depths of 130 feet/40 metres or less). These tables would consider the special needs and circumstances of recreational divers. To this end, in 1983 an avid recreational diver, Dr. Raymond E. Rogers, proposed the development of dive tables for recreational divers. Moreover, Rogers contended that such tables could have significant advantages for recreational divers over the U.S. Navy tables.

Dr. Rogers' rationale for new tables was that the U.S. Navy tables were both too liberal and too conservative for recreational diving. First, he felt that any recreational diving table should reflect more conservative no-decompression limits than provided by the U.S. Navy tables. This was not a new suggestion. Many scientific studies had shown significant "silent bubbling" in divers staying at depth to the full limits of the U.S. Navy tables.

Silent bubbles refer to tiny nitrogen bubbles that occur in the venous (return) circulation. Although their presence can be verified with special detection equipment, these bubbles are apparently too small to cause symptoms of decompression sickness. (As a result, they are referred to as asymptomatic). Normally, these bubbles cause no problems as they are trapped by the minute blood vessels of the lungs. They are then defused and the gas is expelled during the normal respiratory process.

In determining his no-decompression limits, Dr. Rogers used fourteen tissue compartments ranging from 5-480 minutes. However, he found that a tissue compartment no slower than 40-minutes controlled over 90% of all the no-decompression dive profiles reviewed. Nonetheless, some extreme no-decompression profiles did require a slightly slower tissue compartment. So, to cover virtually all profiles, Dr. Rogers chose a more conservative 60-minute compartment as the basis for the surface interval credit table. Because a 60-minute compartment requires only six hours to off-gas completely, the maximum surface interval found on the Recreational Dive Planner is six hours. For added convenience and precision, twenty-six Pressure Group Designators were used to construct the table. The Navy had used fourteen Pressure Groups for their tables.

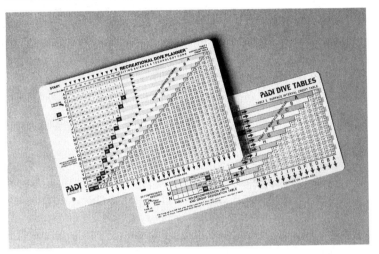

Figure 6-22
A major difference between the RDP and the U.S. Navy Tables is the number of Repetitive Group Designations. The U.S. Navy Tables have fourteen. For greater convenience, the RDP has twenty-six.

Another reason for the development of the Recreational Dive Planner was to enable planning of multilevel dive profiles. This was something the U.S. Navy tables did not take into account. The Navy had designed their tables in consideration of their needs — performing a specific task at a specific depth. However, recreational divers rarely need or desire to remain at a specific depth for the entire duration of a dive. (This is sometimes called a "square profile.") Instead, they dive to varying depths. To meet this need, Dr. Rogers incorporated multilevel capabilities into the his model. This advantage, however, is only possible when using The Wheel, not the Table.

Finally, Dr. Rogers addressed the issue of repetitive dives. Unlike the U.S. Navy Tables, his model provided specifically for three dives in a single day.

Dr. Rogers' concept sparked PADI's interest. A decision was made to fund a project enabling him to refine his concept and test his table model at an independent scientific laboratory. The testing was to consider several important factors not reflected within the U.S. Navy Tables.

First, test subjects were monitored for silent bubbles. Such monitoring is done by an instrument known as a Doppler Ultrasound Bubble Detector. The device works by sending sound waves into the body. The detector is adjusted so that when bubbles are encountered, the sound waves are reflected to a transducer and "heard." The number and degree of sounds detected can be used to determine the

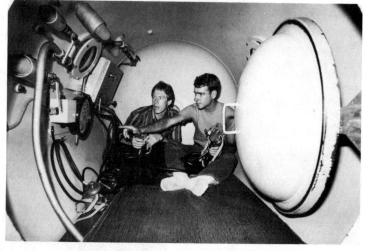

Figure 6-23
The first phase of testing for the RDP was conducted in a recompression chamber.

number of bubbles present. As the technology did not exist in the 1950's, Navy test subjects were not evaluated in this manner. Therefore, because of the technology of the time the Navy was required to use the crude test criterion of "bends/no-bends" to test their tables. Conversely, the Recreational Dive Planner was tested using the more refined criterion of "silent bubbling."

Secondly, the test subjects reflected typical recreational divers in age, physical condition and sex. A profile of the test subjects is provided in Figure 6-24. Since there were no female military divers at the time the Navy developed their tables, only male divers were used in their testing.

Test Subject Profiles

1. Divers: Male: 48 (69%)
            Female: 22 (31%)

2. Age   Male: 32.7 years (range 22-52 years)
            Female: 31.3 years (range 23-44 years)

3. Body Fat (Body Mass Index, Weight/Height^2):
            Male: 22.1%
            Female: 27.4%

4. Average Length of Diving Experience:
            9.7 years (range 1-38)

Figure 6-24

The facility selected to conduct the testing of the Rogers model was the prestigious Institute of Applied Physiology and Medicine (IAPM) in Seattle, Washington. This facility turned out to be an outstanding choice. IAPM is headed by Dr. Merrill Spencer, a pioneer in hyperbaric research. In addition, the primary researcher for the project was Dr. Michael Powell. This was an exceptionally well-qualified team of researchers because Drs. Powell and Spencer were the first to apply Doppler technology to the silent bubbles phenomenon in divers. They also conducted many of the pioneering research studies on silent bubbling.

With a test facility selected, Drs. Rogers and Powell went to work determining the test protocols (procedures, schedules, etc.). Once developed, the preliminary protocols were then sent out for review by other qualified scientists. These scientists included noted researchers such as Dr. Richard Vann at Duke University. After incorporating several suggestions for revision, the testing began in 1986.

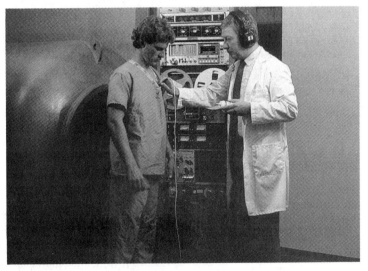

Figure 6-25
After each test dive all test subjects were evaluated for silent bubbles using a Doppler Ultrasound Bubble Detector.

The first phase of the testing took place in the recompression chamber at IAPM's hyperbaric facility. Chamber testing enabled use of profiles which for practical reasons (extreme duration, cold, etc.) are difficult to achieve in open water. The chamber also enabled greater control and safety in the preliminary test phase.

During the chamber dives, the test subjects — all of whom were volunteer divers — were divided into two groups. One group remained at rest during the test dives, while the other group exercised on a rowing machine. After each test dive, every subject was checked for silent bubbles with a Doppler Ultrasound Detector.

Doppler Bubble Grades
Description

Grade	Meaning
0 — no bubbles detected	SAFE
1 — less than 1 bubble per heartbeat	SAFE
2 — 1-5 bubbles per heartbeat	SAFE
3 — 10-20 bubbles per heartbeat	MODERATELY UNSAFE
4 — gas bubbles more numerous than possible to count.	UNSAFE

Figure 6-26

The second phase of testing took place in Puget Sound. Water water temperature ranged from 53 to 55°F/12 to 13°C. In all, the test involved over 911 test dives. This represented the most extensive test ever conducted for the development of repetitive no-decompression dive tables. In fact, it represented four times the number of test dives conducted in the development of the no-decompression portion of the U.S. Navy Tables.

The results of the testing showed not a single case of decompression sickness. In addition, only 1.5% of the non-exercising subjects showed silent bubbling. In the exercising group, silent bubbles were detected in only 4.4% of the subjects. Furthermore, the degree of bubbling that occurred was well within reasonable limits. Doppler bubbles are categorized according to a grade scale contained in Fig. 6-26.

In the non-exercising group, the bubbles detected were all within Grades 1 and 2. In the exercising group the bubbles were also confined to grades 1 and 2, with one single incidence of a grade 3 bubble event.

Rationale for Two Versions of the Recreational Dive Planner

Once the testing was concluded, attention then turned to how the data was to be provided to divers. The problem was how to portray the data in a way that was familiar, yet provided all the benefits of the extensive research. To accommodate both familiarity and maximum benefit, two versions were introduced — a standard table version and a unique Wheel format. A new name was even selected to emphasize the need for dive table consideration being part of every pre-dive plan. The Recreational Dive Planner was born.

The Table is produced for those who want a familiar format. This version provides most of the advantages of the new data, including shorter surface intervals and more conservative no-decompression limits. The procedures for using the Table are exactly the same as for the old PADI Dive Tables. Therefore, divers already familiar with how to use PADI's old tables can immediately use the Table. The primary difference between the new Recreational Dive Planner versus the old PADI Dive Tables is in the number of Pressure Group Designations. The old tables used fourteen Pressure Groups, while the Recreational Dive Planner contains twenty-six. The greater number of Pressure Groups accounts for the larger size of the Recreational Dive Planner over the old PADI Dive Tables. Incidentally, many dive tables use alphabets to designate the status of nitrogen within the divers tissues. However, repetitive groups can never be transferred from one table model to another unless the two tables are based on the same model. Because they are based on the same model, Pressure Groups can be transferred between The Wheel and Table.

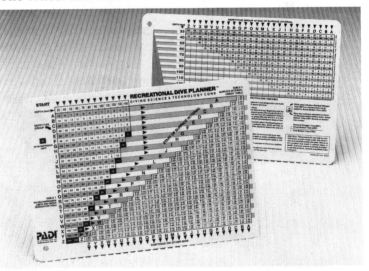

Figure 6-27
The Table was created for those already familiar with how to use the old PADI Dive Tables.

Still, taking full advantage of the new research could be accomplished only by portraying the data in an entirely different way. Rather than the traditional "column-and-row" method, an completely unique method was created — the continuous curve, spiral format of The Wheel. This provides numerous advantages over the more familiar table format. For example, the spiral depth curves allow dive planning down to the minute (tables require increments of several minutes). Also, precision is increased by the five-foot depth increments contained on The Wheel (the tables have 10-foot increments).

Although more precise than the table, the primary rationale for The Wheel was to enable multilevel diving. To minimize the risk of decompression sickness, several safety factors were built into the multilevel diving procedures. These included setting maximum limits to shallower portions of multilevel dives, and providing even more conservative no-decompression limits. Unfortunately, these limitations were difficult to structure into a traditional table format. However, if the decompression status is displayed as a continuous curve, the multilevel limitations can be easily accommodated. The Wheel also provides what is now the only way to do contingency planning when using a dive computer.

Finally, The Wheel is easier to learn and use. When using The Wheel the only factors needed to obtain any information are time and depth. There is no need to consider confusing concepts such as Residual Nitrogen Time and Adjusted No-Decompression Limits. For example, not having to add Residual Nitrogen Time and Actual Bottom Time to determine Total Bottom Time automatically eliminates the single most common error in table calculations. Certainly the greatest advantage of The Wheel is that it is easier to learn and use than the traditional dive tables.

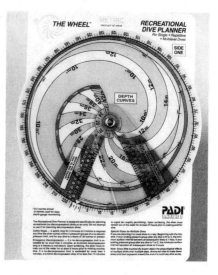

Figure 6-28
The Wheel was created to provide greater precision in dive planning, and to give divers a test way of planning multilevel dives. It's also easier to use than the Table.

Decompression Awareness

PADI Open Water divers are trained on how they can reduce their risk of decompression sickness. They may be unfamiliar, however, with many new scientific and statistical studies that have been done in this field. As a Divemaster, you can be an important source of information and guidance. It is your job to foster a greater awareness of taking responsibility for diving intelligently. The following section is designed to assist you in this role.

Figure 6-29
Plan all dives to reduce the risk of decom-
pression sickness and subsequent
treatment in a recompression chamber.

First, you should make divers aware that they always run the risk of decompression sickness even when adhering to the tables. This is because the mechanisms of decompression sickness are poorly understood. While it is possible to construct dive tables, they are merely mathematical prediction models. No one knows for sure if these models actually mirror what is occurring within the human body. In addition, even if an accurate biological model could be developed, it would still be imprecise because it would reflect the "average person," not the individual. Therefore, even if a physiologically correct decompression model could be developed, it is still unlikely to guarantee complete avoidance of decompression sickness. In essence, the only way to avoid decompression sickness with complete certainty is not to dive.

Other factors also complicate matters. Certain medical conditions and various environmental factors can greatly increase the susceptibility to decompression sickness. How-

Figure 6-30
Prompt in-field treatment — particularly
administration of 100% oxygen — is
essential in cases where decompression
sickness is suspected.

145

ever, as this information is discussed elsewhere, specifics will not be addressed here. For more details on these issues you should read pages 2-27 and 2-28 of *The Encyclopedia of Recreational Diving*.

Table Use Versus Misuse

In addition to biological and environmental factors, divers themselves further complicate the situation by their own behavior and attitudes. Classic examples of inappropriate behavior and poor attitude include: ignoring training guidelines (such as diving beyond recommended limits), totally ignoring the tables, and placing blind trust in a computer. Be certain that divers understand that abandoning common sense and personal responsibility is not the way to avoid decompression sickness.

Still another contributing factor to decompression sickness is the way we dive. Practical experience has shown time and again that certain dive patterns can lead to problems even if such patterns are technically "within the tables." Examples of patterns are that ill-advised include:

1. Sawtooth dives- profiles in which the diver is continually descending and ascending.

2. Bounce dives- making a quick, deep dive after a previous dive.

3. Reverse profiles- beginning a dive at a shallow depth and proceeding to a deeper depth.

Multiple Dives Over Multiple Days

There may be special concerns when making multiple dives over multiple days (sometimes known as "M & M diving"), as is common during diving vacations. Due to concerns over greater than normal nitrogen loading, there are several guidelines divers should abide by when engaged in multiday dive excursions. All are designed to decrease the risk of decompression sickness by conservative use of the tables. These include the following:

1. Stay well within the limits of the tables or computer.

2. Wait 24 hours after diving to fly.

3. Limit the depth on the first dive of the day to 130 feet/40 metres.

4. Limit any repetitive dive to no greater than 100 feet/30 metres.

5. Make a safety stop after every dive.

6. Take a day off from diving on the third or fourth day

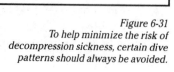

Figure 6-31
To help minimize the risk of decompression sickness, certain dive patterns should always be avoided.

when on a multi-day trip.

7. Avoid making deep dives after shallow dives at any time.

8. Begin each dive at the deepest level — slowly moving shallower as the dive progresses.

9. Heed all rules and warnings for the Recreational Dive Planner regardless of the table or computer used.

Figure 6-32
As very little is known about multiday repetitive diving, divers are wise to take a day off or at least reduce the number of dives toward the end of a trip where you are diving extensively.

These recommendations are not specific to the Recreational Dive Planner. They should be adhered to regardless of the tables or computer being used, especially during multiday trips. In general, advise divers that little is known about the physiological effects of multiple dives over multiple days. It is wise, therefore, to make fewer dives and limit their exposure toward the end of a multiday dive series.

Finally, as a Divemaster you must be aware of the signs, symptoms and in-field treatment for decompression sickness. The key to successful treatment is prompt recognition and action. As a Divemaster such action may fall to you as divers often tend to ignore and even deny symptoms. Therefore, you must be thoroughly familiar with what to look for and how to respond to a possible decompression accident. This information is provided on page 2-28 through 2-31 of *The Encyclopedia of Recreational Diving*. You should review this material before proceeding on to the next section.

Special Rules and Circumstances When Using the Recreational Dive Planner

When using the Recreational Dive Planner several general rules apply. Your duties as a Divemaster require that you be thoroughly familiar with each of these rules. To confirm your understanding of these rules, please review pages 198 and 199 of the PADI *Open Water Diver Manual* before proceeding.

In addition to the general rules of use, certain special rules also apply when using the Recreational Dive Planner. The following section discusses each of these special rules.

Multiple Repetitive Dives

A very special and important circumstance applies whenever a diver using the Recreational Dive Planner plans three or more dives. The rules do not apply if making only two dives in one day. The procedure is as follows:

Figure 6-33
Always remember to take the "Special Rule for Multiple Dives" into consideration when planning three or more dives.

1. If the ending Pressure Group after any dive is W or X, the minimum surface interval between all subsequent dives is 1 hour.

2. If the ending Pressure Group after any dive is Y or Z, the minimum surface interval between all subsequent dives is 3 hours.

These rules assist in reducing the nitrogen loading that results from multiple repetitive dives. Also, as we discussed in the previous section on "Decompression Awareness," divers should always avoid repetitive dives to depths greater than 100 feet/30 metres. This recommendation holds true for using any table or computer. It is an absolute rule when using the Recreational Dive Planner. This maximum depth rule applies even if only two dives are planned.

Safety Stops

For several years "safety stops" have been encouraged before surfacing. These are non-required decompression stops designed to help the body off-gas excessive nitrogen

Figure 6-34
To reduce both the risk of decompression
sickness and lung expansion injury,
encourage divers to take a safety stop at
the conclusion of every dive.

safety stop

before surfacing. This is assumed to reduce the risk of decompression sickness. However, until the introduction of the Recreational Dive Planner, no specific rules have been offered concerning when to make such a stop. As a general recommendation, divers should make a safety stop after every dive. Proper use of the Recreational Dive Planner, however, requires a safety stop when any of the following circumstances apply:

1. After any dive to 100 feet/30 metres (or greater).
2. Any time you will surface within 3 pressure groups of your NDL. (Checking to see whether you are within 3 pressure groups of an NDL should always be your last step when planning a dive.)
3. When a dive is made to any limit of the Recreational Dive Planner.

All safety stops are to be at a depth of 15 feet/5 metres for at least 3 minutes. Also, remember that it is not necessary to add the safety stop time to the bottom time when using the Recreational Dive Planner. (Although you may wish to add the time as yet another safety factor.)

Finally, although safety stops are a good idea, they aren't foolproof. In fact, people differ considerably in their susceptibility to decompression sickness. Therefore, no decompression table can guarantee that decompression sickness will never occur, even though a dive is within the limits of a table. As a result, you should never "push" any tables or computer to or beyond its limits.

Ascent Rates

One of the general rules for using the Recreational Dive

Planner is to ascend no faster than 60 feet/18 metres per minute. This rate was selected and tested because it has long been a standard. Keeping it would therefore not require changes in the way we dive. However, there is nothing wrong with a slower ascent rate. In fact, many believe that a considerable benefit can be gained by slowing the rate below 60 feet/18 metres per minute. While there is no conclusive proof that the slower rate has any bearing on avoidance of decompression sickness, a slower ascent is advised from the standpoint of common sense.

The root of the problem with ascent rates is not in theory but in practice. It has long been recognized that divers tend to ascend at rates much faster than 60 feet/18 metres per minute. Exceedingly fast ascent rates will affect nitrogen off-gassing. Still another problem can arise that is often overlooked entirely — the possibility of a lung overexpansion injury. The sequence of events is simple. The diver begins the ascent neutrally buoyant. During the ascent air within the BCD expands. Upon nearing the surface, the ascent is no longer controlled by the diver, but is actually a buoyant ascent. By this time the rate is likely to be far greater than 60 feet/18 metres per minute.

Figure 6-35
Although a 60 foot/18 metres-per-minute ascent rate is acceptable, slower rates are encouraged. Remember to be a S.A.F.E. diver — Slowly Ascend From Every dive.

Figure 6-36
Duing ascents be especially careful to avoid a buoyant ascent when nearing the surface.

Let's assume further that the diver does not actually hold his breath during this ascent. But, during the last few feet, when the air expansion is greatest, the diver swallows. This action closes off the airway, and is actually a form of momentary breathholding. Now the diver is unknowingly holding his breath while exceeding the proper ascent rate! This combination of events could result in a lung expansion injury.

Since the diver was not aware of holding his breath, the incident could easily be misdiagnosed as decompression sickness, if a problem does occur.

It should be clear by now that slowing the ascent, particularly during the last few feet, is a beneficial practice. To encourage this, PADI has initiated the S.A.F.E. Diver Campaign. S.A.F.E. stands for Slowly Ascend From Every dive, and encourages not only a slower ascent rate, but a safety stop after every dive as well. By planning a stop before surfacing the diver must concentrate on buoyancy control to be able to stop at the 15-foot/5-metre level. The stop, in turn, helps reduce nitrogen levels in the tissues and reduces the likelihood of a lung expansion problem due to rapid ascent. As a Divemaster you should encourage those in your charge to be S.A.F.E. divers.

Emergency Decompression

The Recreational Dive Planner was designed exclusively for no-decompression diving. However, it does provide a contingency if the diver exceeds the no-decompression limit. The specific procedure depends upon exactly how long the diver remained beyond the limit. The following rules will explain how to handle specific situations involving emergency decompression.

1. If a no-decompression limit is accidentally exceeded by 5 minutes or less: Stop for 8 minutes at 15 feet/5 metres. Upon surfacing, remain out of the water at least 6 hours before making another dive.

2. If a no-decompression limit is exceeded by more than 5 minutes: Stop for 15 minutes (or as the air supply permits) at 15 feet/5 metres. Upon surfacing, remain out of the water at least 24 hours before making another dive.

Remember, the Recreational Dive Planner considers any required decompression as an emergency procedure. In addition, never use the Recreational Dive Planner for commercial/military purposes or when breathing a gas other than air.

Omitted Decompression

A procedure also exists if a diver misses an emergency decompression stop. However, unlike some other procedures for omitted decompression, a diver using the Recreational Dive Planner does not reenter the water. Instead, if a diver discovers he has missed an emergency decompression stop, he is to remain on the surface. He should then rest, be alert for any signs/symptoms of decompression sickness and breathe pure oxygen, if available (check local law governing oxygen use). Obviously, seek immediate medical aid if any signs or symptoms of decompression sickness occur.

Figure 6-37
If a required decompression stop is mistakenly missed, never reenter the water. Rest, be monitored for signs of decompression sickness and breathe pure oxygen if available.

With proper dive planning you can easily avoid omitted decompression by planning a safety stop before surfacing. During the stop recheck your bottom time and tables. If you find that you have overstayed the limit, simply remain at the 15-foot/5-metre stop for the additional required time.

Depending on the circumstance, you may encounter divers who subscribe to the omitted decompression procedure used for the U.S. Navy Tables. This involves reentering the water for a series of extended decompression stops at depth from 40 to 10 feet/12 to 3 metres (even deeper in some extreme cases). Actually, this procedure was designed assuming the diver would be in a recompression chamber. As a result its use in recreational diving situations has been in dispute, even by medical authorities, for several years. Currently, the consensus among experts is that recreational divers should not reenter the water under any circumstance if decompression is missed. The procedure established for use with the Recreational Dive Planner should be used regardless of the actual tables used during any no-decompression dive.

Diving at Altitude

Altitude diving at altitude is not specifically a deep diving procedure. But it can result in special decompression problems. For this reason, we will discuss how to use the Recreational Dive Planner at altitude in this section.

Diving at high altitudes requires special techniques

because the diver surfaces to an atmospheric pressure lower than at sea level. The lower surface pressure causes a greater-than-normal difference between the ambient pressure and the nitrogen pressure in the tissues. If this is not accounted for during the dive, the tables will be invalid and cause a greater risk of decompression sickness. For this reason, special procedures must be used when diving and using tables at altitudes above 1000 feet/300 metres.

There has been relatively little high altitude diving research conducted. As a result, whether using a table or dive computer, physiologists recommend very conservative diving practices. For example, it is recommended that divers stay well within the no-decompression limits. A safety stop at the end of all high altitude dives is also an excellent practice.

The following special rules and procedures must be followed when using the Recreational Dive Planner (Wheel or Table) at altitudes ranging from 1000 feet/300 metres to 10,000 feet/3000 metres.

1. Arriving at Altitude: When you arrive at a high altitude destination, you must consider that you have "surfaced" to a lower ambient pressure. You may adjust to this situation in one of two ways. Either wait six hours to adjust to the altitude, or if you want to dive sooner, use the following guidelines. Before you begin diving, determine your pressure group from the change in pressure. At altitude between 1000 feet/300 metres and 8000 feet/2432 metres, count down 2 pressure groups for each 1000 feet/300 metres (round up fractions of 1000 feet/300 metres) from your starting pressure group. You may dive immediately, or allow a "surface interval" to move you into a lower pressure group. Above 8000 feet/2432 metres, wait 6 hours before diving.

For example, assume you are planning a dive in a lake at 4265 feet. Begin by rounding up to 5000 feet. Next, arrival count ten pressure groups to find you are in Pressure Group J before you get in the water. If you elect to wait 1 hour before diving, Side Two of The Wheel, or Table Two of The Table, shows that you have moved into Group C.

2. Rate of Ascent: The Rate of ascent on a high-altitude dive must not exceed 30 feet/9 metres per minute.

3. Repetitive Diving: Make no more than two dives per day when diving at altitude.

4. Depths: To use the Recreational Dive Planner at high altitudes, a depth conversion is necessary. You must first determine your actual depth— the distance you actually are from the surface. This will then enable you to determine

Figure 6-38
Because of the lower atmospheric pressure at altitude, standard dive tables cannot be used in this environment without modification or special procedures.

your theoretical depth — a depth that accounts for the lower pressure at altitude. Use the Theoretical Depth at Altitude table (Fig. 6-39) to convert your actual depth into a theoretical depth for use on the Recreational Dive Planner. You must base all table calculations, no-decompression limits and pressure groups on the theoretical depth. The absolute maximum depth for a dive at altitude is a theoretical 130 feet/40 metres. Always use theoretical depth when calculating with The Wheel or the Table.

For example, assume you are planning a dive to 60 feet in a lake at 4265 feet. Start by finding 60 feet in the left-hand column under Actual Depth. Follow across to the right until you're under the 5000 feet column and read 72. You must treat the dive as if it were a dive to 72 feet. Note that The Wheel's 5-foot depth increments help reduce much of the rounding that is necessary when using the Theoretical Depth at Altitude table. On The Wheel, calculate the dive as 75 feet; on the Table as 80 feet.

5. Safety and Emergency Decompression Stops: Make safety or emergency decompression stops at the depth listed on the Safety/Emergency Decompression Stop Depth table

THEORETICAL DEPTH AT ALTITUDE

Actual Depth	Theoretical Depth at Various Altitudes (in feet)									
	1000	2000	3000	4000	5000	6000	7000	8000	9000	10,000
0	0	0	0	0	0	0	0	0	0	0
10	10	11	11	12	12	12	13	13	14	15
20	21	21	22	23	24	25	26	27	28	29
30	31	32	33	35	36	37	39	40	42	44
40	41	43	45	46	48	50	52	54	56	58
50	52	54	56	58	60	62	65	67	70	73
60	62	64	67	69	72	75	78	81	84	87
70	72	75	78	81	84	87	91	94	98	102
80	83	86	89	92	96	100	103	108	112	116
90	93	97	100	104	108	112	116	121	126	131
100	103	107	111	116	120	124	129	134	140	
110	114	118	122	127	132	137				
120	124	129	134	139						
130	135	140								

©1970 Skin Diver Magazine. Reprinted with permission.

Figure 6-39

SAFETY/EMERGENCY DECOMPRESSION STOP DEPTH

	1000	2000	3000	4000	5000	6000	7000	8000	9000	10,000
Stop Depth	14	14	13	13	12	12	12	11	11	10

Figure 6-40

(Fig. 6-40). Make a three-minute safety stop on all dives. If an emergency decompression stop is required, follow the normal Recreational Dive Planner guidelines for emergency decompression. However, be sure to use the adjusted depths provided on the chart (Fig. 6-40).

For example, at 4265 feet (rounded up to 5000 feet), you make a stop at 12 feet instead of the usual 15 feet. The amount of time at the stop doesn't change.

6. Flying After Diving At Altitude: The rules for flying after diving don't change for flying after diving at altitude. The next section will provide the guidelines for flying after diving.

If driving through mountains immediately after diving, do not ascend to an altitude significantly greater than the altitude of the dive. If, after diving, you intend to drive to a higher altitude than that of your dive, follow the Flying or Driving to Altitude after Diving procedures. Plan your depth conversions for all dives for the highest altitude you will reach.

Finally, here are a few notes on measuring depth. Use of the Theoretical Depth at Altitude table assumes that you are making reasonably accurate measurements of your actual dive depths. When using a depth gauge, keep in mind that many gauges are inaccurate at altitude. However, the design of some depth gauges allows them to be adjusted for use at altitude. Check the manufacturer's literature about the use of your depth gauge at altitude. You may opt to use a marked line and a float to determine depth, rather than a depth gauge. Do not dive unless you can accurately determine your depth.

An oil filled (bourdon tube) depth gauge that is not altitude adjustable will probably show a depth shallower than the actual depth. As a result, it will probable show a depth shallower than the actual depth. The amount of inaccuracy will depend on the altitude. Compare the depth gauge to a depth gauge known to be accurate to determine how many feet off it is.

Capillary gauges always read deeper than the actual depth at altitude. At the start of the dive, the capillary gauge's tube has air in it at the ambient surface pressure. This air pressure is, of course, lower than at sea level. On descent, the water pressure compresses the air within the tube more easily, causing it to read deeper than the actual depth. This also causes the capillary depth gauge to show the theoretical depth, and conversion is unnecessary. When using a capillary gauge limit your dives to shallow water. At deeper ranges (below 30 feet/10 metres) the depth scale becomes increasingly harder to read because of the short

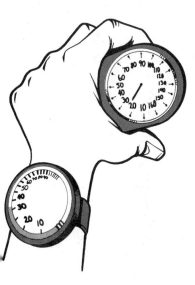

Figure 6-41
Capillary-type depth gauges (left) automatically compensate for use at altitude.

distance between increments.

Flying and Driving to Altitude After Diving

A common post-dive contributing factor to decompression sickness is flying after diving and driving to altitude (such as driving through mountains following a dive). The reason is quite simple. Dive tables are designed assuming that the pressure a diver returns to at the surface is that of sea level (14.7 psia). However, airliner cabins are maintained at a pressure above sea level (usually equivalent to about 5,000-8,000 feet/1500-2400 metres of altitude). That reduced ambient pressure at altitude increases the pressure differential between that within the tissues and the ambient air pressure. The result could be that a diver who might otherwise remain unaffected develops decompression sickness as a consequence of flying.

Figure 6-42
As flying subjects divers to lower-than-normal atmospheric pressures, special procedures should be followed when flying after diving.

Theory aside, the most important factors for the Divemaster to be aware of are the practical guidelines for flying or driving to altitude after diving. According to the most recent guidelines, divers should abide by the following recommendations when going to an altitude between 1000 to 8000 feet/300 to 2400 metres (assuming no symptoms of decompression sickness).

For 1 to 2 days of no-decompression diving: If your total accumulated bottom time for all dives on both days is less than 2 hours, wait 12 hours before going to altitude. For more than 2 hours accumulated bottom time, wait 24 hours.

For more than 2 days of continuous diving, or after any dive requiring emergency decompression: Wait 24 hours.

However, as a general recommendation whenever possible wait at least 24 hours before going to altitude after all no-decompression dives. And whenever possible, wait at least 48 hours after a decompression dive.

Dive Computers

We have already mentioned the use of dive computers in the previous section on "Equipment." However, you must know

Figure 6-43
Divers using computerized
decompression devices are
advised to follow the manufacturer's
instructions very carefully.

more than just how to use these devices. A Divemaster should also have a basic knowledge of how dive computers function, and how their use can affect dive supervision. (You may also wish to review the segment on "Dive Computers" from *Decompression Theory, Dive Tables and Computers).*

To understand dive computers, think back to how dive tables are constructed. Dive tables are actually mathematical models that theoretically describe how nitrogen is absorbed and eliminated by the body. Complex mathematical equations are calculated for the diver and the results displayed in a column-and-row format that cannot be altered. A diver must, therefore, conform to a particular schedule, as determined by the tables.

Today modern computer technology makes it possible to store the complex mathematical equations used as a basis for the tables in the electronic circuitry of a submersible computer. Using various sensing devices, data on depth and time is relayed to the computer throughout the course of the dive. The computer makes the appropriate calculations according to the mathematical model and then displays information on the diver's decompression status.

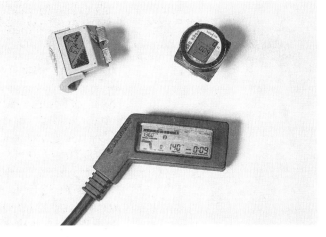

Figure 6-44
Dive computers are the easiest way of
monitoring decompression status — but
they are not a substitute for proper
planning and common sense.

As the diver continually changes depth, so does the information relayed to the computer. The diver receives a constantly changing "status report" on calculated nitrogen absorption/elimination consistent with the model imprinted in the device's memory. With this type of device, the diver no longer needs to fit into the constraints of a table. His decompression status is continually recalculated throughout the dive. Most of all, these calculations are done in consideration of his exact dive profile. Throughout the dive, information is updated and a display shows how long he may remain at a particular depth. Since these calculations must be done frequently (every few seconds), a computer is the only means of accomplish this formidable task.

The Divemaster must also be aware that divers using these devices may appear to "violate" profiles shown on dive tables. While this would normally be a cause for concern, such situations can be explained once we understand the capability of dive computers. A table is static; it cannot continually recalculate data like a computer can. Conversely, a dive computer has the advantage of being able to respond immediately to changes in depth and time, recalculating the equations accordingly.

When supervising divers using computers, the Divemaster should know who is using these devices and caution them to be aware of the information and status of the meter. Should a diver experience a battery failure while using a computer, he should remain out of the water for at least 12 hours. This procedure is necessary because no simple means exists for transferring the diver's decompression status from a computer to a table. In fact, the only way of using a table to plan a contingency for computer failure is to use The Wheel. Then, if a computer failure occurs, the diver can calculate his decompression status for even a multilevel dive.

Figure 6-45
When using dive computers, both buddies should have one, and the more conservative device should be used to determine the decompression status.

(NOTE: Currently, some dive computers are programmed to assume that out-gassing occurs at the same rate as the Recreational Dive Planner. These devices also display a Pressure Group Designation equivalent to those on the Recreational Dive Planner. In this case, if the computer fails, the diver can continue to monitor his decompression status using the Recreational Dive Planner. This, of course, assumes he has recorded the Pressure Group indicated on the computer before it failed. You should check the instruction manual that came with your dive computer to confirm that this is an allowable practice with your particular device).

While dive computers may be the wave of the future, you should encourage divers to avoid blind trust in them. Even the most sophisticated and promising devices have limitations and drawbacks, such as battery failure or mechanical breakdown. Caution divers not to use dive computers without some degree of dive-table planning. The Wheel is particularly well suited for this purpose. By planning the dive in consideration of both the computer and the Wheel, the diver can decide if he wishes to be more conservative than the computer may allow. In addition, he may also have a way to keep a computer failure from ruining an entire day, or more, of diving.

Figure 6-46
The best way to plan a contingency in the event of computer failure is plan the dive in consideration of both the computer and The Wheel. Therefore, if the computer fails, the decompression status can be determined even on a multilevel dive.

Summary

This section has two purposes: 1) to relate information concerning the supervision and control of deep-diving activities, and 2) to discuss in-depth background material relative to constructing and using repetitive dive tables. Both of these vital areas are important to you as a Divemaster and to others who may have supervisory responsibilities.

In the first portion of this section, we discussed the various aspects of equipment, including the selection of personal and supervisory items. We determined that the equipment-selection process of the Divemaster must take into consideration not only his personal needs but also how he may assist others if the need arises. Additionally, because of his special role, the Divemaster cannot afford to use anything other than the very finest-quality equipment.

Next we discussed the important considerations in selecting a deep-diving site. You were cautioned to avoid dive sites with poor visibility, strong currents and exceptional cold. The dangerous practice of diving solely for the purpose of "going deep" was also discouraged.

In the segment on diver assessment we examined the need to carefully consider the divers' experience and anxiety levels. The increased physical demands of deep diving necessitate proper rest and diet. This segment concluded with the need to observe divers during and *after* the dive.

Techniques, such as contingency planning, in-water techniques and diving on walls and dropoffs, were addressed in the segment on "Supervisory Procedures."

The second portion of this chapter involved an extensive discussion of important background information essential to understanding dive tables. Beginning with an overview of the early work done by J.S. Haldane, the section explained the important adaptations made to table design by the U.S. Navy. Next, a thorough explanation on the development of the Recreational Dive Planner was offered, including the theoretical concepts, testing and rationale for the two different formats (the Table and The Wheel).

The next portion — "Decompression Awareness" — explained how new research in the field should effect the way we dive. Guidelines for multiday, repetitive diving were offered, as well as how to avoid inappropriate diving patterns. The importance of diver attitude in avoiding decompression sickness was also discussed.

The section ended on an in-depth discussion of the special rules and circumstances that come into play when using the Recreational Dive Planner. Within this discussion, guidelines were offered on safety stops, emergency and omitted decompression, ascent rates, diving at altitude and flying after diving. The final portion discussed the theory and use of modern dive computers, how plan for a contingency in case of computer failure, and the importance of not placing blind trust in these devices.

Hopefully, this section will enable you and other supervisory personnel to understand the important and complex issues related to deep diving — both in practice and in theory. This knowledge will help you better exercise your responsibility for the safety of others.

Name _____

Date _____

Knowledge Review
Deep Diving Supervision:
Theory and Practice

1. What are some of the most important considerations regarding the selection and use of equipment for deep diving?

_____

_____

_____

_____

2. What considerations are important in selecting an appropriate site for deep-diving activities?

_____

_____

_____

_____

3. What considerations are important in making a proper and thorough assessment of deep-diving participants?

_____

_____

_____

_____

4. What is a *contingency plan* and how may it be most easily constructed?

_____

_____

_____

_____

5. What are the two most vital considerations for the in-water supervision of deep divers? What techniques may be used to assure that these considerations are provided for?

_____

_____

_____

_____

6. How does a *safety stop* differ from a *planned decompression stop?* How should this additional time under water be accounted for in the dive profile?

_____

_____

_____

_____

7. What are some of the unique problems related to supervising divers on walls or dropoffs? How may the Divemaster best respond to these problems?

_____

_____

_____

_____

8. Why is it essential for the Divemaster to have a very thorough knowledge of both the background and use of the dive tables?

_____

_____

_____

_____

9. What was the significance of Haldane's *critical ratio?* How did he account for the differing rate of nitrogen absorption/elimination throughout the body in constructing his decompression model?

_____

_____

_____

_____

10. What was the rationale for the Recreational Dive Planner? Why did the designer consider the U.S. Navy Tables both too liberal and too conservative for sport diving?

_____

_____

_____

_____

11. Why were two versions of the Recreational Dive Planner developed?

_____

_____

_____

_____

12. What special awareness should sport divers have regarding decompression sickness? How does diver behavior and attitude affect their susceptibility to decompression sickness?

_____

_____

_____

_____

13. Why is the ascent rate of special concern in avoiding diving injuries? What can divers do to reduce the risk of problems resulting from ascent rates?

_____

_____

_____

_____

14. Why do special problems result from diving at altitude? What special procedures exist for using the Recreational Dive Planner at altitude?

_____

_____

_____

_____

Notes

Seven

Supervision of Specialized Diving Activities

Section Objectives

☐ **List and explain the function of the specialized equipment necessary for safe participation and supervision of the diving activities discussed in this section.**

☐ **Explain the assessment procedure used to evaluate both divers and diving conditions for the activities discussed in this section.**

☐ **Describe the techniques and procedures by which the activities discussed in this section may be organized to obtain maximum control and safety.**

Introduction

Many diving activities take place in unusual environments requiring specialized equipment and techniques. This often poses special problems for the Divemaster in supervising and controlling these activities. In this section, we will discuss the unique techniques and equipment associated with specialized diving activities relative to the role of the Divemaster and other supervisory personnel.

The specific activities discussed in this section will be: *night diving, drift diving, surf diving* and *cold-water diving.*

165

Figure 7-1
Some more-specialized types
of diving require more-specialized
supervisory techniques.

These activities place special demands on participants *and* supervisory personnel and require an extremely high degree of organization, control and supervision. It is your function as Divemaster to see that these requirements are fulfilled.

This section will not reiterate what has already been discussed in previous sections regarding basic considerations for organization, control and supervision. Instead, we will address the specialized equipment, unique environmental and diver-assessment procedures, and techniques involving each of the listed specialty activities required to obtain maximum control and safety.

Night Diving

This segment is not designed to review night-diving tech-

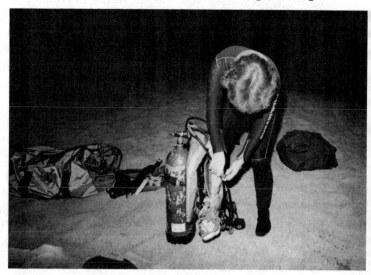

Figure 7-2
Night diving is unique not only for
the specialized equipment it requires,
but also for the unusual psychological
demands it places on the diver.

niques as they relate to the individual diver. For this, review the segment on 'Night Diving' within section Five of *The Encyclopedia of Recreational Diving*. This discussion concerns the *control* and *supervision* of night-diving activities.

Equipment

The Divemaster must consider how his equipment selection will help or hinder the supervision of others. Night diving requires some specialized gear above and beyond standard open water equipment. Night diving requires the use of equipment that may be considered nonessential for other diving activities. Certain equipment — mostly relating to lighting systems — must be available to all supervisory personnel, and all others involved in the dive should be encouraged to use it.

Figure 7-3
A primary light source that is adequate should have at least a six-volt capacity.

All supervisory personnel should have a primary light, designed specifically for underwater use, containing a sufficient power source. Normally, lights with a power source of less than six volts will not provide enough illumination to maintain adequate dive control or to assist others. In particular, lights with wide or ultrawide beams are useful when supervising or directing divers. Surface lights "adapted" for underwater use are often undependable and should not be used.

Occasionally a diver will lose either his light, or its power source, and look to the Divemaster for assistance. Therefore, you or anyone else responsible for in-water supervision should carry at *least one,* if not several, *backup lights.* For convenience, these may be of less power than the primary light. Currently, many small, lightweight lights have been introduced to the diving market and are excellent backup devices.

Figure 7-4
Many smaller, less-obtrusive lights are excellent backup devices.

An effective light source, other than a dive light, should be made available for use on the surface. Dive lights should be restricted for use under water. Lanterns are especially well-suited for surface operations. Most dive boats have deck-lighting systems that fulfill this purpose. Use of underwater lights for surface preparation is a tremendous and needless waste of battery power.

Chemical glow-lights are effective in maintaining group supervision and you should require all divers in your charge to carry one. These lights enable one's buddy and supervisory personnel to maintain visual contact with divers even if the primary dive light fails. Additionally, chemical lights are now available in a variety of colors. When possible, you

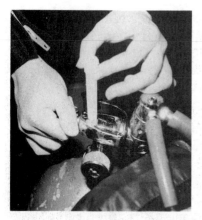

Figure 7-5
All divers should be required
to attach a chemical glow-light
to their person or equipment.

Figure 7-6
Underwater strobes are well-suited
for signaling the entry/exit area,
but should never be used above water.

and other supervisory personnel should be assigned a different color than that used by other divers. Using different colors will allow a quick and immediate distinction to be made between *divers* and *supervisors,* even while in the water and at a distance.

The exit point should be well marked with a light to facilitate the divers' return. An effective means to mark the exit area is with a continuous flashing underwater strobe. There are many units available now that, when used under water, may be seen for considerable distances. These devices provide underwater direction finding and orientation capabilities to the divers. Additionally, using strobes can give a sense of security to otherwise anxious divers by providing reassurance that safety is only as far away as the strobe light. One important word of caution is that strobe lights should never be used *above* water because they may be interpreted as navigational aids or distress signals. Caution should be exercised when using underwater strobes because they may attract stinging jellyfish or similar marine life.

As a final word of warning regarding equipment requirements, in some instances, buddy teams have been allowed to share a *single* light during a night dive. This can cause a severe control problem because the failure of only *one* light can affect the safety of *two* divers. Such a *one-light-for-two* practice should never be allowed. *Every* diver should be required to have his own light source, and backup lights should be encouraged.

Assessment Procedures

Environmental-assessment procedures for night diving are no different then at any other time. However, dive-site familiarity becomes especially important at night. Under no circumstance should the Divemaster plan a night dive in an area with which he has no previous experience. Complete familiarity, made possible only through extensive daylight experience at the site, is essential for effective control of night-diving operations.

When you are selecting a dive site, you should avoid areas with strong currents, extreme depth or adverse environmental conditions. Additionally, because of the convenience it affords divers and because it makes dive supervision easier, night dives should be conducted from a boat whenever possible.

Diver-assessment procedures are essentially the same for night diving as at all other times. Night diving will,

Figure 7-7
When night diving, the Divemaster should conduct a thorough area orientation — even if the site is already familiar to the divers.

however, tend to be more stress-inducing than daylight diving. Even experienced divers who are normally calm and at ease may become anxious and frightened when diving at night. Regardless of experience, all divers bear special observation during night dives. You should also consider the relative experience level of those diving together when pairing divers. When possible, try to pair inexperienced night divers with those who have experience. You should be particularly careful not to allow peer pressure to force a reluctant diver to dive.

Finally, when you are making a diver assessment, be sure to take their personal equipment adequacy into consideration. In addition to making sure that divers are using the proper dive lights, encourage divers to wear appropriate exposure suits or protective clothing (especially in tropical areas to protect against stinging marine life and coral abrasions); encourage them to use compasses, low-pressure BCD inflators; and suggest gauges with luminescent dials.

Night-Diving Planning and Procedures

Relative to supervision and control, there are several important techniques unique to night-diving activities. The following suggestions should serve as a guide to the Divemaster involved in the organization, control and supervision of a night dive.

Figure 7-8
Even in tropical environments, complete exposure protection is advised.

Determining *when* to dive is dependent upon several considerations like logistical and environmental factors. The dive objective and diver experience level can also have an important bearing on decision making. Particularly with inexperienced divers or for training activities, night dives

Figure 7-9
Deciding on whether to schedule a night dive in the early or late evening will depend on logistics and the dive objective.

should be planned for soon after sunset. At this time, ambient light present will illuminate the water as the divers enter. As the dive progresses, the gradual decrease in light will allow time for divers to become accustomed to the environment. This procedure can aid greatly in decreasing the stress often associated with night diving.

To an experienced diver, a later dive may be more enjoyable — particularly if diving in an ocean environment. Waiting until later in the evening (several hours after sunset) allows time for the change from a daytime to a nocturnal environment. Marine life that is active at night is often totally different than that seen during the day. However, diving soon after sunset does not allow time for the transition to complete. The decision of when to dive should depend upon the objective and experience level of the group.

Although dependent upon the personnel available, supervision of a night dive is usually best accomplished from the surface. From a high vantage point on the surface — usually the bridge or bow of a boat — the Divemaster can easily observe the progress of the dive by watching for lights or groups of lights in the water because the *lome* or glow of dive lights can be seen from a considerable distance on the surface (depending on depth and visibility). Should you decide to dive with the group, as always, make sure *competent* supervision remains on the surface at all times.

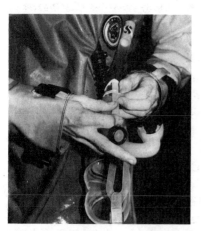

Figure 7-10
Supervisory personnel — especially the Divemaster — should attach their chemical lights to their snorkels.

Those assigned to surface supervision should decide how they would respond in the event of a problem. If rescuers are dispatched, they, too, must have a means to denote their location in the water. Therefore, a chemical light should be attached, though not activated, to the *snorkel* of all supervisory personnel. The light should never be attached to the tank assembly because in some instances, the tank may need to be abandoned. Depending upon the situation, a rescuer dispatched from a boat or from shore may not don a tank at all, though he should always take his mask and snorkel.

To provide easier control for the Divemaster and easier orientation for the divers, a down line should be rigged to facilitate descent. This line may be marked at intervals with chemical lights for easy identification. Using a down line will also provide an increased sense of security and reassurance to the divers by giving them guidance to the bottom. When diving from a boat, the anchor line may serve as a down line, but a guide line rigged from the entry point to the anchor line is also helpful.

During your pre-dive briefing, you should communicate the following night-diving techniques guidelines to the divers:

1. *Monitor air consumption, time and depth more closely than normal.* Due to excitement, diving at night typically causes divers to consume air faster, and the lack of visual perspective (due to the darkness) can give divers a false sense of depth. (In-water supervisory personnel should pay close attention to diver air consumption.)

2. *Maintain good buoyancy control.* The lack of perspective mentioned in item No. 1 can easily result in an uncontrolled descent. Proper buoyancy control is also essential in remaining comfortably *off* the bottom. This is especially important to avoid *silting* of the bottom, or when ocean diving, to avoid sea urchins and other hazards.

3. *Caution divers not to attempt to cover as much area as they may during the day.* This advice will help reduce the divers' energy expenditure and allow the surface supervisor to more easily observe divers in the water. It is also not *necessary* to cover as much area at night because of the novelty of the environment and the inability to see a great distance. In fact, if an underwater strobe is used, the divers may wish to stay within the range of the strobe's light throughout the entire dive.

During the briefing, the Divemaster should also mention a few words concerning entries and exits at night. Divers should be instructed to turn their lights on *prior* to entry so that in the event a light is accidentally dropped overboard, it can easily be retrieved. Warn divers to avoid shining their lights in the eyes of surface supervisors or boat crew during the exit.

Figure 7-11
Not only should a descent line be used at night, but it should be well-marked with chemical lights or strobes.

Figure 7-12
When night diving, divers should be advised to confine their activity to an area not too distant from the exit.

Figure 7-13
Drift diving is an extremely enjoyable and efficient way of diving, but it requires close supervision and specialized techniques.

Drift Diving

Drift diving has numerous definitions. In the context of this section, drift diving will mean *any form of diving done in moderate to heavy current in which the exit point is significantly downstream of the entry point.* Drift diving is a highly specialized activity that can be either boat- or land-based.

The advantages of drift diving are numerous and include: a significantly decreased level of energy expenditure (as one is floating or swimming *with* the current); the ability to cover a tremendous area during the dive; and the ability

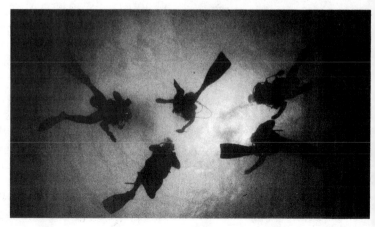

Figure 7-14
Effective supervision of a drift dive requires that the group remain close together throughout the dive.

to dive in areas where *anchor diving* is not advised or even possible.

When you are supervising a drift dive, there are numerous problems unique to this type of diving of which you should be aware. Most importantly, the group needs to remain together at all times to facilitate control. Divers must remain close to each other during all phases of the dive from descent to ascent. Drift diving is best done from a boat to make organization easier; in this case, the boat may be adrift or *live* (under power).

Equipment

Specialized equipment for drift diving is helpful in maintaining group control. For each *group* of divers, the recommended equipment includes an adequate surface float and colored polypropylene line. Each *diver* should have a whistle or other signaling device to enable him to signal for assistance if he gets separated from the group.

Because the float provides a reference point for the group, it must be buoyant enough to remain afloat even if all divers in the group hold on to it for support. Additionally, the float denotes the in-water location of the group to supervisory personnel on the surface and must therefore be highly visible. Probably the item that best fulfills all of these requirements is a large (18-inch/46-centimetre diameter minimum), international orange fender buoy (tear-drop shape) that is available in most marine-supply stores. It provides ample buoyancy, visibility and easy attachment of the down line. Many areas have laws that require divers to display the appropriate diver-down flag. The Divemaster must be certain that his surface float complies with the appropriate laws.

Figure 7-15
Use of the proper surface float / descent-line system will enable the Divemaster to exercise greater control.

The down line is the group's link with the surface. The line should be strong but of a manageable size. A minimum diameter of eighth-inch/.32-centimetre polypropylene line is good for this purpose because it is colorful (usually yellow or blue) and can be seen easily by all divers; it is strong and can resist the force of several divers pulling on it; and it is easily managed. The line may be wound upon a large plastic spool and paid out as needed or used without a spool. When used, the spool end often contains a loop to facilitate handling or a clip that allows you to attach the spool to your belt, enabling you to use both hands to assist divers without losing contact with the line.

Supervision Procedures

While adequate surface supervision is necessary when drift

diving, competent in-water supervision is also required for each group involved in the dive. Generally, in-water group size should be limited to six to eight divers, including the supervisor. All group members must be cautioned to remain close to the down line at all times. The Divemaster may also require those with little drift-diving experience to maintain physical contact with the down line throughout the dive. Your decision to require contact with the line will be dependent upon the strength of the current, group size, depth of the dive and experience level of the participants.

Because drift dives are typically conducted in deeper environments like underwater walls, you must carefully consider your underwater positioning relative to the group. You should usually be at the very bottom of the group and positioned in a manner that enables you to watch both the divers

Figure 7-16
The Divemaster usually controls the depth of a drift dive by positioning himself at the very bottom of the line.

and the down line. The object of such positioning is to prevent divers from descending deeper than the dive plan allows and to prevent the line from becoming entangled. In other instances, you may choose to remain in shallower water to more closely supervise inexperienced divers. As with determining proximity to the float, the deciding factors in determining your underwater position should be the depth of the water, the size of the group and the experience level of the participants.

Entry-and-Descent Procedures

When a group of divers enters the water, the most important entry procedure to advise them of is to have them enter the water *in very close succession* so the divers will not become separated upon descent. The supervisor should be first to enter the water, with the down line and float, so he may lend any needed in-water assistance.

Figure 7-17
One of the keys to effectively controlling a drift dive is making sure divers are able to enter the water as quickly as possible.

Usually the most problematic portion of a drift dive is the descent. There are two techniques of descent that you may use, and deciding which one to use is dependent on the specific environment and the experience level of the participants. The first technique requires the group to, upon entry, assemble and remain on the surface until you instruct them to descend. This is usually the most appropriate technique with inexperienced divers or with those who may still be in training. In using this technique, however, separation is likely if divers descend before you direct them to do so, but it allows more time for the divers to prepare for the descent. Close supervision is therefore essential while on the surface. This technique is advised only if the dive does *not* have to be initiated in a very specific location.

The other entry-and-descent technique is used when the dive *must* be initiated in a very specific spot. In this instance, the descent must be made *immediately* upon entry to avoid being swept away from the desired location. To accomplish this, divers should enter the water *without* air in their BCDs so they can quickly begin the descent. You can easily pay out the down line while you are descending. During their descent, the other divers can maintain contact with the line to control their rate of descent. Divers should continue to watch for directions from you as they descend. The entire process requires a high degree of readiness and precision, although with practice it is easily executed. Still, this technique is suggested only with relatively experienced divers and in situations where quick and immediate descents are essential.

Whatever descent technique is used, you should be particularly alert for divers experiencing difficulty in equalizing. Divers experiencing difficulty with equalization (and their buddy) should be instructed to halt their descent but *remain*

Figure 7-18
To aid descent, a common procedure for drift diving is for divers to enter the water without *air in the BCD.*

Figure 7-19
Upon reaching the bottom, the Divemaster
should confirm that everyone is accounted
for and allow the divers to acclimatize.

in contact with the descent line so that they will not become separated from the group. You may then either provide assistance to the diver experiencing difficulty or take whatever action necessary to return the diver to the surface. Your decision will again depend upon the depth, size of the group and their experience level.

Upon reaching the bottom, you should account for all divers before proceeding. Next, allow divers to *acclimatize* and regain normal respiration. Also, be sure you confirm the direction of the current since the direction of the underwater current can *differ* from the direction of the surface current.

Dive Termination and Exit Procedures

Throughout the dive, the Divemaster should periodically check his air supply and communicate this information to the others. This practice will encourage other divers to monitor their own air supply and avoid a possible out-of-air emergency.

Particularly in deeper water, the dive must be terminated

Figure 7-20
Usually a drift dive is terminated when
the first diver reaches 500 psi/40 bar of
air, so the Divemaster must closely
monitor the air consumption of the group.

176

when the *first* diver reaches the minimum allowable air pressure (usually not less than 500 psi/40 bar). At this time, you should attract the other divers' attention and signal the group to *immediately* ascend. It may take a few moments to attract everyone's attention, so no time should be wasted in initiating the ascent. *Everyone* must ascend, regardless of how much air remains in their tanks. You should always be the last one to ascend so that you will be in the best position to observe the others.

This termination procedure may be altered somewhat when diving in shallow water. In this case, provisions are occasionally made to allow divers running low on air to ascend first, in teams or with other supervisory personnel, and remain on the surface in contact with the float. Because this procedure could sacrifice some degree of control, it should be used with caution and only with experienced divers or in very shallow water. Supervisory personnel on the surface should also be informed of this procedure so that it is not interpreted as a problem situation.

Once on the surface and ready to exit, the group should establish positive buoyancy and maintain *very close* proximity to the float. Divers should also give an *OK* signal to the boat to confirm that all is well. At this time, the vessel will begin its approach toward the group. This point can be very hazardous because the vessel will be under power. You must maintain complete control and provide specific directions to those in the water.

During the surface phase of a drift dive, it is crucial for you to coordinate closely with the vessel. The vessel will usually approach from downwind to avoid being blown into

Figure 7-21
A safe, efficient exit requires
close coordination with the boat.

the divers. You should instruct the divers not to swim toward the vessel until directed to do so, because the captain will take the vessel out of gear before taking the group aboard. Once instructed, the group should exit the water as usual. You should remain in the water to offer any assistance.

In drift diving, as the group is diving independent of a fixed reference point, the Divemaster's utmost consideration is control and supervision of the divers.

Surf Diving

Often surf diving is considered to be a completely unique and highly specialized form of diving. This concept is inaccurate because surf diving differs little from any other type of

Figure 7-22
The only "specialized" aspect of
surf diving is entry and exit.

diving except for *entry* and *exit* considerations. Once through the surf, the diver must contend with the same factors and variables as at any other time.

Prior to involvement in surf diving supervision, you should have a basic understanding of what causes surf and its various characteristics. For this, a review of the segment entitled "Waves" from *The Encyclopedia of Recreational Diving* and the segment entitled "Ocean Diving" from the PADI *Open Water Diver Manual* is suggested.

To the Divemaster, the supervision of surf diving essentially involves control and assistance to those divers in the surf zone. Once out of the surf zone, control and supervision considerations are no different than in other diving activities.

Assessment

Making an informed decision regarding surf conditions requires familiarity and knowledge. The Divemaster's primary

Figure 7-23
Determining the relative difficulty
of surf-diving conditions is not easy,
because divers often have differing
backgrounds and ability levels.

consideration should be whether the diving participants are capable of dealing with the conditions present. This is a question not easily answered, because you may not be familiar with all the divers, and their abilities and experience levels may vary greatly.

During the briefing, you should evaluate the experience level of the participants. Special provisions should be made to ensure that inexperienced surf divers are closely supervised during the entry and exit. If possible, experienced divers should be paired with those who have less experience.

Procedures

Often surf diving can be controlled through onshore supervision, particularly if the activity does not involve training. Onshore supervisors should, however, be prepared to enter

Figure 7-24
When supervising surf-diving
activities from shore, the Divemaster
should be constantly prepared to
enter the water to lend assistance.

the surf zone to lend assistance. When the need arises for the onshore Divemaster to enter the water, quick action and balance will be essential. Onshore supervisory personnel must therefore be continually ready to enter the surf zone to

179

provide assistance. This readiness will require that they be equipped properly in order to function once they enter the water. Obviously, such capabilities require a high degree of familiarity and practice and should be attempted only by those with considerable experience in surf diving.

If sufficient supervisory personnel are on hand, a more direct and effective means of maintaining control is to have these individuals actually accompany the group during the dive. In-water supervisors should be cautioned to exercise particular care when transiting the surf zone and be prepared to lend assistance at a moment's notice. Additionally, you should always review basic surf-diving techniques during the dive briefing. The specific entry technique used will depend upon the conditions and the divers' individual experience levels. Of particular importance are the following:

Entry Considerations

1. Advise divers that all equipment adjustments should be made *prior to entry* to enable them to move through the surf zone as quickly as possible.

2. Caution divers to coordinate their activities to *move with the motion of the water.* Attempting to move against wave action and surge is exhausting and fruitless.

3. Because the key to safe surf entry involves submerging as soon as possible, advise divers to have only a minimal amount of air in their BCDs. This will facilitate the time-

Figure 7-25
The key to a successful surf entry is being
fully prepared *prior to entering the water.*

Figure 7-26
Advise divers to avoid establishing
too much buoyancy while in the surf zone.

consuming procedure of deflating the BCD. Additionally, substantial positive buoyancy caused by a fully inflated BCD can cause the diver to be picked up and thrown by breaking waves.

4. If a diver falls, he should be instructed to *stay down*

and never attempt to regain footing in the surf zone. It is far easier to continue the entry while crawling or swimming.

Exit Considerations

Divers should also be made aware of several considerations related to exiting through surf:

1. At the end of the dive, prior to reentering the surf, divers should surface and wait just outside the surf zone. This allows time for the divers to rest and evaluate conditions (remember that surf conditions may change *during* the dive).

2. Once the exit begins, instruct divers to remain submerged as long as possible when exiting. This prevents

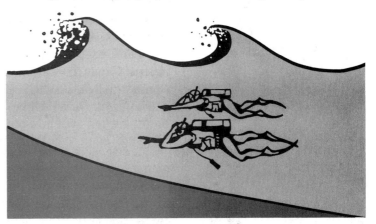

Figure 7-27
When exiting surf, divers should be advised to try to remain submerged as long as possible.

them from being picked up and thrown by the breaking waves. Care should be exercised not to establish an excessive amount of buoyancy at this time.

3. Instruct divers to keep all equipment in place and to reserve enough air so that the exit can be made while breathing from the *scuba unit* (snorkels are very difficult to keep clear in surf).

4. Should the diver fall while walking out of the water, he should be instructed *not* to get up. Divers should instead

Figure 7-28
Advise divers who fall during entry or exit to crawl or swim — never stand — when trying to resume the activity.

continue swimming and, if necessary, crawl out of the water.

Surf diving is not difficult and differs from other forms of diving only in the entry and exit procedure. With practice, supervision and control of surf diving is actually quite simple if the proper guidelines are followed.

Cold-Water Diving

To consider cold-water diving a specialty may seem unusual to many divers. But, the majority of all diving activity takes place in moderate temperatures (usually above 70°). Most divers do not have experience in water so cold that the temperature becomes a significant factor.

Cold water is a relative term. What may be considered cold to one diver may easily be considered pleasantly mild to another. Generally, diving in water temperatures below 70° is considered cold-water diving. Regardless of formal definition, virtually all diving takes place in an environment well below normal body temperature. Therefore, all divers must be concerned with how body heat is dissipated during a dive.

This segment is designed to provide guidelines and procedures for supervising and controlling diving activities in cold-water environments and deals *only* with technique. To become more familiar with the physiological and environmental effects of cold, review the segment entitled "Physiological Responses to Thermal Changes" in section Two of *The Encyclopedia of Recreational Diving.*

This segment will not deal specifically with ice-diving techniques. Though most of the information presented here is highly applicable, ice diving should be considered a specialized form of diving requiring an equally specialized degree of training. Those interested in ice diving should seek out a PADI Ice Diver specialty course.

Avoiding Hypothermia

The number one concern that serves as a guideline in supervising cold-water diving activities is avoiding hypothermia. Successfully avoiding hypothermia requires proper exposure protection, adequate pre-dive rest and diet, and a recognition of the debilitating effects of cold water on the diver.

Proper exposure protection not only relates to how the diver is dressed in the water but *out* of the water as well. A primary contributing factor to the onset of hypothermia in divers is that they often *begin* the dive in near-hypothermic states, and the situation worsens as the dive continues. Regaining body heat while under water is virtually impossible;

Figure 7-29
Choosing exposure protection depends not only on water temperature, but on personal preference as well.

Figure 7-30
Proper exposure protection is also important for those who will be supervising diving activities from the surface.

the key is to *prevent heat loss* both during *and* before the dive.

Divers should dress warmly and consider the topside environment. Caution divers to always wear more clothing than they think will be necessary and to wear several layers rather than a single heavy garment. Layering allows for adjustments in the amount of exposure protection. Having extra clothing on hand will provide divers with ample additional protection once they are out of the water and is also useful if the divers' other clothing becomes wet. Also, caution divers not to stand in exposed, windy areas prior to diving because this can cause considerable pre-dive heat loss. Individuals involved in surface supervision should wear warm clothing to protect against the long hours spent in the open.

Figure 7-31
A primary cause of heat loss in divers is failure to conserve heat prior to diving.

Exposure Suits

For in-water protection, divers will be wearing either wet or dry suits. A wet suit can be perfectly adequate even in very cold water, if the garment fits well and is properly designed. A quarter-inch suit with Farmer John pants and cold water (wide bib) or attached hood should be considered the minimum acceptable dress for cold-water activities.

There are numerous techniques that may be used to aid divers in preventing pre-dive heat loss. Provisions should be made for divers to be able to don their exposure suits in a protected (ideally, heated) location. If divers are going to be wearing wet suits, an effective preventative technique is to "preheat" the suit by pouring warm (not hot) water into it just prior to the dive. Also, remember that wet suits are designed to work *in the water.* Once divers are out of the water, the moistened surface of their wet suits will quickly dissipate their body heat through convective cooling. Divers should be encouraged to change back into dry clothing as soon as possible after exiting the water. If another dive is planned, have them remove their wet-suit top and replace it with a dry, warm jacket or sweatshirt during the time of the surface interval.

Figure 7-32
"Preheating" the wet suit with warm water is an effective means of reducing heat loss upon entry.

By far, the best garment option for cold-water diving is the dry suit. Recent developments in lightweight nylon suits provide maximum warmth without sacrificing maneuverability. The undergarments worn beneath these suits are specially designed for extreme environments and help keep the diver warm both in *and* out of the water. While more effective than a wet suit, dry suits do require the diver to

Figure 7-33
Lightweight-fabric dry suits offer
excellent thermal protection without
sacrificing maneuverability.

Figure 7-34
Special consideration must
be given to rescue procedures
when diving in cold environments.

have some additional experience. These suits are designed to be inflated, so divers must be aware of the resulting changes in buoyancy. Divers using dry suits should be properly trained in how to use them, and this is one reason that dry suits should be purchased only from a reputable dealer.

Supervisory Considerations

As noted in a previous section, large groups will require adequate surface supervision. This requirement presents a dilemma in cold environments. Because surface supervisors must dress warmly, it will not be possible for these individuals to enter the water quickly if necessary. Provisions should therefore be made for a standby rescuer to be prepared to immediately enter the water if needed. Ideally, this role should be alternated throughout the dive to prevent hypothermia of a single diver.

The Divemaster must be particularly observant during cold-water diving activities because of the gradual and insidious nature of hypothermia. Shivering is certainly an important sign in determining the state of the diver. Shivering is only temporary, however, and it will quickly *cease* if the diver's body temperature continues to drop. Another sign of the onset of hypothermia is a pronounced reduction in manual dexterity, though this may be difficult to determine because divers are likely to be wearing bulky gloves or mittens. The final and most potentially dangerous sign of hypothermia is a decrease in awareness and reasoning ability. While this is, to say the least, a hindrance while on the surface, it is life-threatening under water. The astute Divemaster must be constantly vigilant and pay particular attention to any divers showing signs of decreased capability or awareness.

Summary

In this section, we discussed the unique supervision and control requirements for night diving, drift diving, surf diving and cold-water diving. This section also provided you with guidelines on proper equipment, dive logistics and diver-assessment procedures. To give you sufficient background to prepare divers for these diving activities and to enable you to anticipate common problems, we reviewed some important, relevant techniques.

Supervising specialized diving activities is an especially important role for you as the Divemaster. These diving ac-

Figure 7-35
Supervising specialized activities requires
considerable training and experience.

tivities often take place in unique and potentially hostile environments in which participants rarely have extensive experience.

Epilogue

The purpose of this manual was to present information to those responsible for supervising divers in how to *control* and *manage* diving activities. The manual was also designed primarily as a text for the PADI Divemaster Course, one of the most extensive professional training programs in existence.

Generally, the approach of the manual moved from very broad to very specific. This was accomplished in the first section entitled "Orientation and the Role of the Divemaster" by considering the varied and extensive functions that a Divemaster may be required to fulfill. The second and third sections were devoted to general considerations relative to *planning, management* and *control.* But, the information presented in these sections is applicable to virtually all diving activities. The fourth section described the Divemaster's responsibility in *dealing with student divers* and hopefully provided a valuable perspective on becoming an instructor. The remaining portion of the manual addressed how the general guidelines covered in the previous sections could be applied to very specific activities. These activities included *boat diving, deep diving* and a wide array of *specialized activities* ("Supervision of Specialized Diving Activities").

Additional Opportunities

Satisfactory completion of the PADI Divemaster course is an especially important milestone in a diver's career because it qualifies him for membership in the PADI association. This professional certification should, however, be considered

Figure 7-36
The PADI Divemaster rating is the first
step in becoming a diving professional.

only an interim step in becoming a fully certified PADI Open Water Instructor.

In terms of continuing professional education, the next step for you as a qualified PADI Divemaster is the PADI Instructor Development Course (IDC). This course is unique to the diving industry. Due to its extensive array of support materials and completely standardized curriculum, the course is able to concentrate upon creating effective business-minded educators.

PADI IDCs are available throughout the world and may be completed in either a seven-consecutive-day format or conveniently scheduled like most other diving courses. A complete informational brochure on the PADI Instructor-development process is available from either PADI Headquarters or from a local PADI 5 Star Instructor Development Center. It is advisable for people interested in attending an IDC to obtain an *IDC Candidate Workbook* from a local 5 Star Instructor Development Center. The workbook is a valuable resource and provides a thorough overview of what is contained in the IDC itself.

Figure 7-37
Consider the Divemaster rating but one step on the path to becoming a fully certified PADI Instructor!

The recreational diving industry can offer outstanding opportunities to capable men and women, and is a great means to turn one's interest in diving into an exciting full- or part-time profession. As a qualified PADI Divemaster, you are well on your way to realizing this dream.

Name _____

Date _____

Knowledge Review
Supervision of Specialized Diving Activities

1. What specialized equipment, and procedures for its use, are useful in supervising night-diving activities?

_____

_____

_____

_____

2. What are the most important considerations in making a proper and thorough assessment of the dive site and the participants of night-diving activities?

_____

_____

_____

_____

3. List and explain several procedures relative to *planning* that are unique to night diving.

_____

_____

_____

_____

4. What techniques are useful for night-diving *supervision?* What guidelines concerning technique should be communicated to *divers* prior to night diving?

_____

_____

_____

_____

5. What specialized equipment and procedures for its use are important in supervising drift-diving activities?

_____

_____

_____

_____

6. What are the most important considerations in supervising a drift dive?

_____

_____

_____

_____

7. What two different procedures may be used during the descent phase of a drift dive? Under what circumstances would either procedure be used?

_____

_____

_____

_____

8. What are the procedures for terminating a drift dive? How may this procedure differ in shallow as opposed to deep water? What are some important considerations if divers are to exit onto a boat?

_____

_____

_____

_____

9. What are the general procedures suggested for supervising surf-diving activities?

_____

_____

_____

_____

10. What basic guidelines concerning entries and exits should be communicated to divers prior to engaging in surf diving?

_____

_____

_____

_____

11. What pre-dive procedures can a diver follow to help avoid hypothermia while diving? What features or techniques can optimize the use of a wet suit in cold water? What are some important consideration regarding the use of a dry suit?

_____

_____

_____

_____

12. What special supervisory problems does cold-water diving present? What signs should the Divemaster be alert for in other divers that could signal the onset of hypothermia?

_____

_____

_____

_____

Appendix

Answers to Knowledge Reviews One

1. PADI Divemaster Training differs from other levels of PADI diver training in that it is the first step in becoming a diving *professional*. As a result, the Divemaster rating carries with it a substantial amount of *responsibility for others*.

2. The minimum prerequisites for PADI Divemaster Training are that the candidate must hold a PADI Rescue Diver certification and be 18 years of age or older. Additionally, the candidate must have a high degree of emotional maturity, physical stamina and diving ability. The goals of PADI Divemaster Training are detailed on page 3.

3. Module One of the PADI Divemaster course is designed to assess and provide remedial training in the areas of watermanship, general diving skills, diver-rescue techniques and the ability to deal with stress-inducing problems.

Module Two is designed to increase the candidates' knowledge of the theory and principles of diving, specifically in the areas of diving physics; diving physiology; equipment; diving skills and environment; the dive tables; and first-aid procedures.

Module Three is designed to inform candidates of the diver-training process, typical student problems and how to supervise and control divers in general.

4. A Divemaster may fulfill the following functions:

- An underwater *guide,* which is the most typical role.
- An out-of-water *supervisor* of diving activities.
- An *instructional assistant* to a qualified instructor.
- A *medic* who can provide first aid in the event of an emergency.
- An *oceanographer* who can answer questions concerning the environment and it inhabitants.
- A *technician* responsible for maintaining and repairing equipment.
- A *counselor* who helps other divers deal with stress.
- A *public-relations expert* responsible for ensuring divers an enjoyable experience.
- A *seaman* who is responsible for, or aids in, the safe operation of a dive boat.
- Finally, because the Divemaster is so specially trained to deal with others, he is a *trained buddy* — probably the most qualified individual one can dive with.

5. The benefits of PADI Membership are:

   1. Free subscription to *The Undersea Journal*
   2. Updates to PADI Standards* and programs
   3. Availability of low cost professional liability insurance; and
   4. Special prices on various PADI products.

Refers to the "Standards and Procedures" section of the Instructor Manual.

Two

1. The two essential components of dive planning for the Divemaster are *familiarization* and *assessment*.

2. A high degree of familiarity with divers *and* the dive site is essential for the Divemaster to make informed decisions concerning the conduct of the dive. Becoming familiar with divers may be accomplished through prior experience, while thorough dive-site familiarity can best be accomplished through construction of an underwater map as detailed in the section on Dive Planning.

3. The Divemaster may *indirectly* assess those divers in his charge through astute *observation* of equipment and behavior. In terms of equipment, the Divemaster must assess the general condition and style of the various items to determine their suitability. In terms of behavior, the Divemaster must assess the divers' apparent degree of familiarity with equipment and procedures; signs of stress and the effect of peer pressure; overdependence upon a spouse or diving buddy; and the amount of time taken to complete preparations.

4. The Divemaster may *directly* assess those divers in his charge through informal discussions, as long as he makes certain that he does not offend them. In such discussions, the Divemaster may wish to establish the divers' certification level; amount and type of previous diving experience; significant medical considerations; and a general impression of the individual's psychological condition.

5. It may be difficult at times for the Divemaster to accurately determine the acceptability of the environmental conditions present at a dive site because the concept of *acceptability* is relative; what may be acceptable for one individual may be totally unacceptable for another. Also, in most recreational settings divers usually have highly varied backgrounds and experience levels, thus further complicating the situation.

6. Generally, weather information may be obtained from newspaper, television and radio reports, though more specific marine-oriented reports are often available. The U.S. and many other countries broadcast this information on VHF-FM frequencies. Other sources may include reports from airports or other marine authorities.

7. In coastal areas, due to the unequal heating of the ocean and adjoining land masses, convection currents often develop. This condition gives rise to onshore winds that gradually intensify as the day progresses. Coastal winds will therefore tend to be lightest during early-morning hours — normally an ideal time for diving activities.

8. Divers are typically affected by *localized* currents caused primarily by *tidal exchange*. In areas where currents are particularly significant and apt to have a considerable effect on the diver, dives should be planned during the period of *slack tide* — the point at which there is minimal tidal flow.

9. A diver caught in a strong current should be advised *not* to attempt to fight the current. Instead he should be advised to establish positive buoyancy, to rest and to drift with the current. The Divemaster can then dis-

patch assistance to retrieve the individual without fear of the diver becoming exhausted.

10. The factors that can affect underwater visibility, and therefore have great consequence on dive planning, are as follows:

*   *Weather* and *seasonal variation* affect the amount of particulate suspended in the water, such as rain and plankton.
*   *Bottom composition, wave action* and *surge* are especially significant when the bottom is prone to easy disturbance.
*   The *time of day* is important in determining how much sunlight will penetrate the water's surface.
*   Major *oceanic currents* and the physical *location* of a dive site are factors that determine large-scale weather patterns.

11. While the opportunity to see marine life is one of the prime motivations for diving, the real or imagined danger from marine life is also a primary concern for divers. The function of the Divemaster is to help the diver strike a balance between these two conflicting view points, thus allowing divers to enjoy the experience of diving while conveying a realistic understanding of the potential dangers of marine life.

12. The guidelines a Divemaster may follow to help protect the marine environment are detailed on page 33.

Three

1. Relative to supervising diving activities, *control* is the ability to prevent or immediately respond to a problem in order to avoid discomfort, injury or panic. The essential elements of control include: *preparation, communication, positioning* and *recognition*.

2. Six equipment items useful in managing and controlling large-scale diving activities are:

1. A clip board and roster (ideally the PADI Dive Roster) for maintaining information and diver-accounting procedures
2. A first-aid kit
3. Oxygen
4. A flotation device to facilitate any rescue attempt
5. Communications and signalling devices to enable contact with both divers in the water and emergency personnel
6. Maintenance and convenience items (such as a *save-a-dive kit*)

3. Within the *area orientation* portion of a dive briefing, the Divemaster should relate information concerning:

*   The general characteristics of the site
*   The depth range
*   Any special entry or exit considerations or techniques
*   Buddy-team assignments (if necessary)
*   A review of general safety rules (PADI Safe Diving Practices), communications (such as hand signals), and appropriate emergency procedures

4. During the dive briefing, the important considerations for the pre-dive safety check can easily be remembered by the memory device *Begin With Review And Friend.* This will cue the recall of the BCD *B,* weights *W,* releases *R,* air *A,* and final OK *F.* The specifics to look out for during the safety check are outlined on page 52.

5. To be considered adequate, an accounting procedure must provide for the following information:

   1. The name of every diver involved in the activity
   2. Buddy-team assignments
   3. Entry and exit times
   4. Information on maximum depth, bottom time and surface interval*

6. The general guidelines the Divemaster should use in planning effective in- and out-of-water supervision are:

   1. Determining the proper vantage point from which to oversee activities
   2. Having the appropriate equipment on hand to effectively manage and control the dive
   3. Being adequately prepared to respond to a diver should the need arise

7. The most often-overlooked aspect of out-of-water supervision is *readiness for response.* This aspect requires the Divemaster to make provisions for *immediately* rendering aid, and, therefore, the duty should not be handed over to untrained people.

8. In-water supervision should only be attempted if:

   - considering all environmental factors, the group is of sufficient size to enable everyone to dive as a single group

   OR

   - there are already enough supervisory personnel on hand to maintain adequate surface supervision.In-water supervision should not be attempted in lieu of surface supervision if more than one group of divers is involved in the activity.

9. In determining the proper positioning for in-water supervision, the Divemaster must consider the following:

   1. Which diver is most likely to experience difficulty?
   2. At what point or location during the dive will problems be most likely?
   3. What effects will environmental conditions have?
   4. What is the Divemaster's function during the dive?

10. In terms of dive supervision, the emergency procedures of primary importance are *buddy separation, out-of-air emergencies* and the *recall of divers.* Most of the problems associated with these situations may be avoided through proper communication prior to the dive. Also, the in-water supervisor should pay particular attention to divers' air supply and should be equipped with an alternate-air-source device.

*Using computerized decompression devices may alter this requirement.

11. PADI Instructors, Assistant Instructors and Divemaster *Members* are qualified to conduct PADI Environmental Orientation dives and issue the appropriate decal. Any certified diver is eligible to participate in these dives.

12. Green — indicates a dive made in a freshwater environment.
Blue — indicates a dive made in an ocean environment (water temperature below 70°F/21°C).
Red — indicates a dive made in an ocean environment (water temperature above 70°F/21°C).

Four

1. The duties of an instructor are all-encompassing, but his most important role is *teaching*. The duties of the Divemaster, on the other hand, involve *supervision* of those not under the direct control of the instructor, and *assisting* the instructor in his teaching capacity.

2. The functions a Divemaster may fulfill relative to diver training involve:
   1. Supervision of both entry-level and continuing education students
   2. Consulting with the instructor concerning student attitudes and performance
   3. Handling logistical matters and other preparatory activities
   4. Serving as a *role model* to students

3. According to PADI Standards,* a *certified assistant* is defined as a PADI Divemaster, Assistant Instructor or Instructor (no others qualify). During PADI Open Water Diver courses certified assistants may escort tours only after students have completed all skills evaluations with a qualified PADI Instructor. A certified assistant may *not*, however, independently supervise the tour for experience during Open Water Training Dive No.1. Only a certified PADI Instructor is qualified to supervise this first experience tour. When conducting independent experience tours during Open Water Training Dives 2-5, PADI Standards stipulate that the Divemaster supervise not more than two students at a time. This ratio changes when supervising students in the Continuing Education course. Refer to the PADI *Instructor Manual* for details on supervising Continuing Education training activities.[1]

4. The term *professionalism* requires that the following criteria be fulfilled:
   - Possess a specialized expertise.
   - Follow a prescribed standard of practice.
   - Remain up-to-date with the state of the art in the profession.
   - Have ethical and impartial conduct toward students and other divers.
   - Have an appearance that conveys the proper respect and attitude toward the profession.

5. In terms of training activities, a *proper attitude* for the Divemaster requires:

*Refers to the *Standards and Procedures* section of the *Instructor Manual*.

- a philosophical agreement with the instructor and the PADI System concerning the conduct of training
- an acceptance of the need for consistency and adherence to training standards
- empathy and concern for others, particularly students
- appreciating the need for encouraging students to acquire proper diving equipment

6. Concerning pool-training activities, the Divemaster's function is to:
   - Supervise student skill development (after initial instruction by a qualified instructor) and provide input.
   - Enforce ground rules and observe students to ensure that all activities are conducted in a safe manner and location.
   - Assist or conduct equipment distribution, preparation and suiting-up activities.

7. During open-water training, the Divemaster's function as a surface supervisor involves overall logistical charge of the dive site. He should be responsible for equipment preparation, check-in/check-out procedures, coordinating entries and exits and generally handling any problems that may arise on the surface or out of the water. Fulfilling these duties allows the instructor to concentrate entirely upon the evaluation of student performance.

8. *Positioning* is a particularly important element of control when dealing with students because students have little or no previous diving experience. This fact requires the Divemaster to maintain very close proximity to students while in the water and to pay careful attention to students who are not under the direct observation of the instructor.

9. *Problem recognition* is a particularly important element of control when dealing with students. Because of their lack of experience and higher anxiety levels, students typically make mistakes that would not be expected of more-experienced divers. Most importantly, a Divemaster who is especially alert and attentive should decrease the likelihood of problems or decrease the severity of consequences if problems occur.

10. The two aspects of problem recognition are:
    1. The *proper response* to problems should they occur
    2. The *prevention* of problems

Five

1. Generally, the factors that determine the type of boat used for diving activities in any given location are related to the the type of environment present (how much protection must be provided from the elements) and the relative distance to the dive sites (how long divers must be aboard). Areas with large diver populations usually have fleets of boats specifically designed for diving, while less-popular areas often require the use of fishing or pleasure craft to do double duty as dive boats.

2. Legal requirements relative to operating a dive boat involve the vessel *and* its operator. The operator must have the appropriate license (accord-

ing to the number of passengers carried and size of the boat). The vessel may need to be certified (according to the number of passengers to be carried) and have the appropriate safety equipment (which varies according to the size and design of the vessel).

3. Equipment that is relative to diver safety and not necessarily required by law includes: *oxygen* (ideally capable of being delivered at 100% concentrations); *first-aid kit; appropriate dive flags; stern line and float; chase boat or rescue board;* and some form of *diver-recall device* or procedure. Dive boats should also have an acceptable means for allowing divers to enter and exit the water, and all crew members should have at least a rudimentary knowledge of boat-diving procedures.

4. A general guideline to follow for any Divemaster who may be acting as a crew member aboard a dive boat is that he should possess the capability to temporarily take charge of the vessel in the event the captain is incapacitated. This may involve actually running the vessel or simply being able to properly and efficiently summon assistance.

5. A knowledge and familiarity with nautical charts can be very helpful to the boat-based Divemaster for several reasons. Detailed charts may provide vital information about the dive site, enabling a better assessment of environmental factors. Additionally, should an emergency arise, authorities can best be directed to the site when an accurate position is determined from a chart.

6. There are several avenues by which a Divemaster may receive information concerning potentially hazardous situations at sea. *Storm warnings* are posted at all Coast Guard facilities and harbormaster offices; *continuous weather broadcasts* that broadcast weather-related hazards are available, and *notices to mariners* are broadcast, posted or may be obtained from local Coast Guard officials.

7. The type of radio that should be used for on-board communications is a VHF-FM marine radio. The radio is, however, *only* to be used for communications of a *safety* and *operational* nature (not for socializing). The various protocols set up to monitor transmissions make this radio particularly useful in an emergency, and all Divemasters should become familiar with these procedures (detailed on pages 99-100).

8. In terms of docking the boat, a Divemaster who is also acting as a crew member will be expected to follow the instructions of the vessel's captain. Generally, the Divemaster should keep divers clear of any area that may place them in danger or interfere with the docking maneuver. He should also be fully prepared to fend off the vessel from the dock or other obstructions, be able to properly handle docking lines, and confirm the security of the vessel once it has been docked.

9. A Divemaster acting as a crew member must prepare the anchor prior to arriving at the site so that it may be dropped immediately upon word from the captain. The anchor should be dropped well upwind from the dive site and in consideration of how not to damage the underwater environment (particularly coral reefs). Once it is clear that the anchor has hit bottom, it must be confirmed that the anchor is holding. Raising the

anchor involves maneuvering the vessel to efficiently break the anchor free from the bottom. This action will require the Divemaster to carefully direct the captain in how and where to position the boat. The key is to make the vessel do most of the work instead of "muscling" the anchor back aboard.

10. The Divemaster's pre-dive procedure should include:

- passenger check-in and gear-stowage familiarization
- an orientation to the vessel
- a review of certain on-deck rules
- a review of emergency procedures
- an orientation to proper entry/exit procedures

11. When diving from a boat, the Divemaster should instruct divers to:

- Maintain a position *in front* of the vessel at all times (by taking a compass bearing or periodically ascending to check position).
- Be back on board with 300-500 psi/20-40 bar of air remaining in their tanks
- Give the *OK signal* to the boat upon surfacing.
- Use the stern line for assistance if caught behind the vessel.

12. When supervising diving activities from a boat, the Divemaster or other responsible individual must be attentively positioned as high above the water as possible to facilitate observation. Particular attention should be paid to divers who are on the *surface* and/or *behind* the vessel, although even the underwater location of divers may be determined from bubble trails. Most importantly, the Divemaster must be capable of *immediate* response should a problem be identified.

13. During the exit and post-dive phase of the dive, the most important considerations are:

- Allow only one diver at a time to board the exit ladder and warn others to stay well clear.
- Prepare to immediately lend assistance.
- Ascertain the divers' bottom time and maximum depth.
- Remind divers to avoid cluttering the deck with discarded equipment.
- Visually confirm that everyone is aboard before departure.
- Observe divers for delayed response to diving-related problems (such as decompression sickness).

14. Specific techniques to help avoid seasickness are contained on pages 114-115.

Six

1. When selecting equipment, the Divemaster must remember that he may be required to remain in the water longer than others and may be called upon to lend assistance. He should therefore use only top-quality equipment. Generally, the guide to equipment selection should be to have more air and warmth available than is thought necessary. A balanced regulator, some form of alternate-air-source device, a high-quality timing device and a depth gauge are minimum personal essentials. Safety and communications/information equipment is also required.

2. The Divemaster should plan deep-diving activities only in locations where he has significant previous experience. He should avoid areas with strong currents and poor visibility. He should also give special consideration to water temperature — particularly because it may affect the selection of exposure suits.

3. The primary factor in assessing deep-diving participants is their level of prior experience. Ideally, those making their first deep dive should be under instructor supervision, though a Divemaster may be considered an acceptable substitute. The Divemaster should be alert for signs of anxiety and provide an easy out for anyone who may not wish to dive. As deep diving places considerable physical demands on the divers, they should be encouraged to eat properly and get sufficient rest prior to diving. The Divemaster should also continue his assessment even *after* a deep dive because there is an increased possibility of decompression sickness.

4. A *contingency plan* is a predetermined plan of action the dive team will follow if some unforeseen factor, such as going deeper or staying longer than anticipated, should occur. Portions of the PADI Repetitive Dive Work Slate were designed to assist in constructing contingency plans.

5. The two most vital considerations for in-water supervision of deep divers are:

1. The increased density air at depth will require divers to expend considerably more air and energy than normal.
2. The narcotic effect of the increased partial pressure of nitrogen will cause divers to become less aware of themselves and their surroundings. To overcome this, the Divemaster should:
   1) maintain very close proximity to the divers;
   2) control the descent of the group (usually through use of a down line);
   3) be alert for abnormal behavior in the divers and
   4) continually monitor the divers' air supply.

6. A *safety stop* differs from a planned decompression stop in that it is not required, according to the tables, to avoid decompression sickness. They are simply a safety measure. The procedure calls for divers to stop prior to surfacing at a depth of *5 meters/15 feet* for *at least 3 minutes*. It is not necessary to add additional time spent under water to the bottom time of the dive.

7. Diving on underwater walls or *drop-offs* is usually accompanied by very good visibility. Therefore, divers may easily descend deeper than planned and be otherwise lulled into a false sense of well-being. The Divemaster has two courses of action in maintaining control of the dive:

1. *Lead* the group while requiring it to maintain very close proximity to him

OR

2. *Remain behind* the group but at a good vantage point from which to observe.

The Divemaster's objective in both cases is to assure that divers do not descend below the prescribed depth. Divers should also be cautioned to maintain good buoyancy control during the dive.

8. The Divemaster must have a very thorough knowledge of both the background and use of the dive tables because:

- He must often make important safety-related decisions concerning depth, bottom time and surface intervals.
- He will be looked to as the expert by other divers who have questions concerning the tables.

9. In Haldane's model of decompression, his *critical ratio* (1.58) represented the maximum amount of nitrogen pressure within the tissues, above the ambient pressure, that could be tolerated without developing decompression sickness. He compensated for differing rates of absorption/elimination by dividing the body into five theoretical *compartments,* each with its own presumed rate of absorption/elimination.

10. Dr. Rogers rationale for Recreational Dive Planner was that the U.S. Navy Tables, although used successfully for many years, were not designed for recreational diving applications. He believed the tables were too liberal because they allowed longer no-decompression limits than were indicated by Doppler Bubble Detector studies. He also believed the U.S. Navy Tables to be more conservative than necessary because they imposed needlessly conservative surface interval times between repetitive dives. Selecting the 120-minute tissue compartment on which to base the Surface Interval Credit Table was appropriate and necessary for the Navy. But for no-decompression, repetitive diving, as done by recreational divers, a much faster controlling tissue compartment could be used. In the case of the Recreational Dive Planner, a gas wash-out tissue compartment of 60-minutes was selected to control repetitive diving.

11. Once testing was concluded, it was decided to portray the Recreational Dive Planner data in two different formats. The Table was produced for those who wanted a familiar format. The use procedures for the Table are exactly the same as for the old PADI Dive Tables. Therefore, divers already familiar with how to use PADI's old tables could immediately use the Table of the Recreational Dive Planner. However, to gain full advantage of the new research the data had to be portrayed in an entirely different way. Rather than the traditional "column-and-row method," a continuous curve, spiral format of The Wheel was developed. This provided numerous advantages over the traditional table format including more precision and multilevel planning capabilities. The Wheel is also easier to learn and to use than the Table.

12. All divers should be aware that, because we know little about the physiology of decompression sickness, they always run the risk of decompression sickness even when adhering to the tables. Even if a physiologically correct decompression model could be developed, it is still unlikely to be able to guarantee complete avoidance of decompression sickness. Certain medical conditions and various environmental factors can greatly increase the susceptibility to decompression sickness. In addition, inappropriate behavior and poor attitude — such as ignoring training guidelines, ignoring the tables all together, and placing blind trust in a computer — also contribute to decompression sickness. Certain dive patterns also contribute to decompression sickness. These dive patterns can lead to problems even if such patterns are technically "within the tables." Exam-

ples of patterns are that ill-advised are "sawtooth profiles," "bounce dives," and "reverse profiles." There are also concerns when making multiple dives over multiple days. There are several safety guidelines divers should abide by when engaged in multiday dive excursions. These are contained on page 146-147.

13. Many believe that considerable benefit can be gained by slowing the ascent rate below 60 feet per minute. Because of lack of buoyancy control awareness, divers commonly exceed the 60 feet per minute rule. As a result, the practice of taking a safety stop at the conclusion of every dive is advised. This helps off-gas excess nitrogen and helps avoid possible lung overexpansion problems that are more likely near the surface. To encourage slower ascents, PADI has initiated the S.A.F.E. Diver Campaign. This encourages not only a slower ascent rate, but a safety stop after every dive as well. By planning a stop before surfacing the diver must concentrate on buoyancy control to be able to stop at the fifteen foot level. The stop, in turn, helps reduce nitrogen levels in the tissues and reduces the likelihood of a lung expansion problem due to rapid ascent.

14. Diving at high altitudes requires special techniques because the diver surfaces to an atmospheric pressure lower than at sea level. The lower surface pressure causes a greater-than-normal difference between the ambient pressure and the nitrogen pressure in the tissues. If this is not accounted for during the dive, the tables will be invalid and cause a greater risk of decompression sickness. For this reason, special procedures must be used when diving and using tables at altitudes above 1000 feet/300 metres.

When using the Recreational Dive Planner at altitudes greater than 1000 feet/300 metres, be sure to follow the procedures outlined on page 152 through 155 with respect to: arriving at altitude, ascent rate, repetitive diving, depth calculation, safety and emergency decompression stops.

15. Procedures recommended for flying after diving are listed on page 156.

Seven

1. Specialized equipment useful in the supervision of night diving includes:
   - An underwater light with sufficient power and beam angle to provide assistance to others
   - Backup lights (the more the better)
   - A surface lighting source other than that to be used under water
   - Chemical glow-lights to mark the in-water location of divers
   - A light (ideally a strobe) to mark the unnderwater location of the exit

2. In making a proper and thorough *dive-site assessment* for night diving the Divemaster should select only a location that is familiar to him. Environments with strong currents, extreme depth and generally adverse conditions should also be avoided. A boat should be used for night diving whenever possible. *Diver assessment* should take into consideration the higher anxiety levels associated with night diving and the adequacy of personal diving equipment.

3. In planning a night dive, special attention should be given to the time of night the dive is to be made. Earlier dives (beginning around twilight)

are advised for inexperienced divers or those in training. Diving at twilight allows divers to acclimatize to the gradual decrease in light. More experienced divers may, however, prefer a later dive because this will allow time for a changeover from day-to-nighttime marine life to occur.

4. Supervisory night-diving techniques include the need for:
   - Competent surface supervision
   - Pre-decided emergency procedures
   - A *down line* to aid descent

Divers should be informed of the following night-diving techniques:

   - Monitor air supply more closely than normal (because of probable increased air consumption).
   - Maintain good buoyancy control (due to possible disorientation and silting).
   - Do not attempt to cover as much area as when diving during the day (to facilitate supervision and maintain proximity to the exit).

5. The most important piece of specialized equipment useful in supervising drift diving is the *down line.* The down line is used to mark the location of a dive group while in the water. This line should include an adequate surface float (such as a large international-orange fender buoy), a minimum 1/8-inch/.32 centimetre polypropylene line and possibly a spool (with a clip or lanyard) that allows the supervisor to easily control the line.

6. Supervising a drift dive requires keeping the size of the group to a manageable number, depending upon diver experience and environmental factors. Greater control may be afforded if divers are required to maintain contact with the down line, though this may be needlessly restrictive in some cases. The supervisor should probably be positioned nearest the bottom to control the depth of the dive. However, the primary consideration in terms of positioning should be the ease with which divers may be observed and directed.

7. When diving with inexperienced divers or entry-level students, or if the descent point is not of critical importance, the descent may be initiated after everyone has assembled on the surface. The Divemaster must be careful not to allow the group to be dispersed by the current, however. With more experienced divers, or when the descent point is critical in order to arrive at a very specific part of the dive site, the descent should be made *immediately* upon entry (no air in the BCD). Regardless of which technique is used, the supervisor should always be the first one in the water. The group must always follow in quick succession.

8. A drift dive is usually terminated when the first diver in the group reaches a predetermined level of air (normally about 500 psi/40 bar). At that time, the *entire* group should *immediately* ascend under the direction of the supervisor, who is the *last* one to ascend. In shallower water, or with more experienced divers, an alteration of this procedure is allowable. In this instance divers may be allowed to ascend independently in teams as they begin to run low on air. Ascending divers should be cautioned to remain near the surface float. Surface supervisors on shore or aboard the boat should also be forewarned about this procedure so that they will not interpret it as a problem. When exiting onto a boat, the supervisor must maintain extremely close control over the group. Divers must remain in

close proximity to the float and not approach the vessel until instructed to do so.

9. Surf diving is often best controlled by having a *surface supervisor* ready to lend assistance to divers in the surf zone. If sufficient supervisory personnel are on hand, however, they may be assigned to each dive team (or at least the most inexperienced) and may be prepared to offer assistance if needed.

10. Guidelines on entries and exits to be communicated to participants of surf-diving activities are listed on pages 180-182. These should be reviewed at the dive briefing, especially to the inexperienced.

11. To avoid hypothermia when diving in extreme environments, divers should be cautioned to try to retain as must body heat as possible *before* entering the water. This can best be accomplished by dressing warmly in several layers of clothing. Adequate rest and diet are also important. When using a wet suit in cold water, it should be of sufficient thickness (¼-inch) with Farmer John pants and a wide bib or attached hood. The suit can be filled with warm water prior to entry. Once out of the water, wet suits will cause the diver to dissipate body heat very quickly. Although dry suits are considerably warmer and therefore much better for colder environments, they do require training and familiarity prior to initial use.

12. Special problems are presented to those responsible for surface supervision of cold-water activities. While the surface supervisor must dress warmly, this will normally prevent him from readily entering the water in the event of an emergency. Therefore, a *standby* diver is often used to provide assistance if needed. Whether in or out of the water, the Divemaster must be aware and alert for signs indicating the onset of hypothermia. These signs may include:

- Severe shivering (though temporary)
- Decreased manual dexterity
- Decreased awareness and reasoning ability

Generally, the Divemaster must be on guard for any behavior that could indicate impairment due to cold.

PADI® ACCIDENT MANAGEMENT WORKSLATE

ATTENTION: Physicians and Emergency Medical Personnel

The individual identified on this slate has been involved in scuba diving activities and may have suffered a pressure-related injury resulting from decompression sickness or lung overexpansion. You have no reason to be familiar with all the pathological details of the various rare disorders which may occur. It is, however, imperative that you follow the guidelines outlined *in the red box on the reverse side of this slate* until arrival at a medical facility.

In addition, the Divers Alert Network (DAN) at Duke University Medical Center is prepared to assist you in patient treatment. DAN may be contacted at **(919) 684-8111.** A physician experienced in the management of diving accidents is available for consultation.

Victim's Name _____ Age _____

Address _____

Contact: _____ Phone: ( )_____
　　　　　☐ Relative　　　☐ Friend

SIGNIFICANT MEDICAL HISTORY: (allergies, medications, diseases, injuries, etc.)

_____

_____

_____

SIGNS/SYMPTOMS: (note time)

FIRST AID PROCEDURES INITIATED: (note time)

DIVE PROFILE:

First Dive	Second Dive	Third Dive
Time In _____:_____	Time In _____:_____	Time In _____:_____
Time Out _____:_____	Time Out _____:_____	Time Out _____:_____
Depth _____:_____	Depth _____:_____	Depth _____:_____

COMMENTS: _____

_____

_____

_____

_____

PADI® DIVING ACCIDENT MANAGEMENT FLOWCHART

IF AN ACCIDENT OCCURS:

1. Locate patient's I.D., and recent diving history.
2. Use reverse side of this slate to record information as indicated.
3. Secure patient's gear. Rinse and hold, do NOT disassemble.
4. Upon proper identification, cooperate with authorities.

5. Make only factual statements; do NOT make value judgments or express opinions.
6. Write accident report as soon as possible while events are fresh.
7. **Send this slate and other appropriate information with evacuation personnel.**

Has the individual taken a breath under water from a compressed air source?

NO → Not a diving accident. Go to nearest hospital.

YES →

Mild Symptoms
Fatigue   Skin Rash
Itching

NO →

Serious Symptoms

Unusual weakness
Pain (particularly joint, abdominal, and lower back)
Dizziness, vision or speech difficulty
Paralysis, numbness/tingling
Breathing difficulty
Severe cough
Bloody, frothy mouth
Decrease or loss of consciousness
Convulsions

YES →

1. Administer oxygen (100% ideal).
2. Have patient lie level on left side, head supported.
3. Administer nonalcoholic fluids, such as fruit juices, orally.
4. Observe for more serious symptoms.
   RELIEF WITHIN 30 MINS.?

YES →

Keep patient under observation and consult diving physician as soon as possible.

NO →

1. Maintain open airway — prevent aspiration of vomitus.
2. Initiate CPR if necessary.
3. If conscious/breathing independently, administer oxygen (100% ideal).
4. Have patient lie level on left side, head supported.
5. Advise patient not to sit up during first aid or transport.
6. If convulsion occurs, do not restrain — support head/neck.
7. Protect injured diver from excessive heat, cold, wetness, noxious fumes.
8. If conscious, administer nonalcoholic fluids, such as fruit juices, orally.
9. Arrange immediate evacuation to appropriate medical facility.
   NOTE: DO NOT DISCONTINUE THESE FIRST AID PROCEDURES EVEN IF PATIENT SHOULD SHOW SIGNS OF IMPROVEMENT.

© International PADI, Inc. 1991

EMERGENCY	Ambulance/Medical _____	Diving Physician _____	Police _____
CONTACT	Medical Facility _____	Chamber _____	Other _____
INFORMATION	United States: DAN (919) 684-8111 USGC VHF Channel 16		

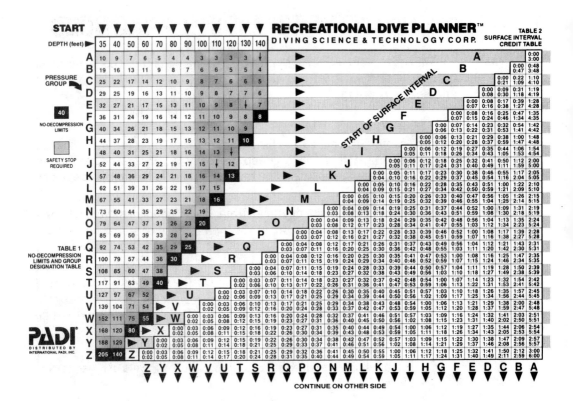

RECREATIONAL DIVE PLANNER™
DIVING SCIENCE & TECHNOLOGY CORP.
TABLE 2 — SURFACE INTERVAL CREDIT TABLE
TABLE 1 — NO-DECOMPRESSION LIMITS AND GROUP DESIGNATION TABLE

START — DEPTH (feet) — PRESSURE GROUP — NO-DECOMPRESSION LIMITS — SAFETY STOP REQUIRED — START OF SURFACE INTERVAL

CONTINUE ON OTHER SIDE

PRESSURE GROUP AT END OF SURFACE INTERVAL

TABLE 3 • REPETITIVE DIVE TIMETABLE

(White numbers = Residual Nitrogen Time, RNT, in minutes)

DEPTH (feet)	Z	Y	X	W	V	U	T	S	R	Q	P	O	N	M	L	K	J	I	H	G	F	E	D	C	B	A
35	205	188	168	152	139	127	117	108	100	92	85	79	73	67	62	57	52	48	44	40	36	32	29	25	19	10
40	140	129	120	111	104	97	91	85	79	74	69	64	60	55	51	48	44	40	37	34	31	27	25	22	19	10
50			75	67	63	60	57	53	50	47	44	41	38	36	33	31	29	27	26	24	21	19	17	16	14	7
60				54	52	49	47	44	42	39	37	35	33	31	29	27	26	24	22	21	19	17	16	14	11	5
70									38	36	34	33	31	29	27	26	24	22	21	19	18	16	15	13	11	5
80										29	28	26	25	23	22	21	19	18	17	15	14	13	11	10	8	4
90											24	23	22	21	19	18	17	16	15	13	12	11	10	9	7	4
100													19	18	17	16	15	14	13	12	11	10	9	8	6	3
110																15	14	13	12	11	10	9	8	7	6	3
120																		12	11	10	9	8	7	6	5	3
130																					9	8	7	6	5	3

The Recreational Dive Planner is designed specifically for planning recreational (no-decompression) dives on air only. Do not attempt to use it for planning decompression dives.

Safety Stops — A safety stop for 3 mins at 15 ft is required any time the diver comes within 3 pressure groups of a no-decompression limit, and for any dive to a depth of 100 ft or greater.

Emergency Decompression — If a no-decompression limit is exceeded by no more than 5 mins, an 8-min decompression stop at 15 ft is mandatory. Upon surfacing, the diver must remain out of the water for at least 6 hrs prior to making another dive. If a no-decompression limit is exceeded by more than 5 mins, a 15-ft decompression stop of no less than 15 mins is urged (air supply permitting). Upon surfacing, the diver must remain out of the water for at least 24 hrs prior to making another dive.

Flying After Diving Procedures — 1) For 1 to 2 days no-decompression diving: If your total accumulated bottom time for all dives on both days is less than 2 hrs, wait 12 hrs before going to altitude. For more than 2 hrs accumulated bottom time wait 24 hrs. 2) For more than 2 days of diving, or after any dive requiring emergency decompression: Wait 24 hrs. Whenever possible wait at least 24 hrs before going to altitude after all no-decompression dives.

Diving at Altitude — This planner is not designed for use at altitudes greater than 1,000 ft above sea level.

Special Rules for Multiple Dives
If you are planning 3 or more dives in a day: Beginning with the first dive, if your ending pressure group after any dive is W or X, the minimum surface interval between all subsequent dives is 1 hr. If your ending pressure group after any dive is Y or Z, the minimum surface interval between all subsequent dives is 3 hrs. *Note: Since little is presently known about the physiological effects of multiple dives over multiple days, divers are wise to make fewer dives and limit their exposure toward the end of a multi-day dive series.*

General Rules
- Ascend from all dives at a rate not to exceed 60 ft per min.
- When planning a dive in cold water or under conditions which might be strenuous, plan the dive assuming the depth is 10 ft deeper than actual.
- Plan repetitive dives so each successive dive is to a shallower depth. Limit repetitive dives to 100 ft or shallower.
- Never exceed the limits of this planner and whenever possible avoid diving to the limits of the planner. 140 ft is for emergency purposes only, do not dive to this depth.

White area indicates Residual Nitrogen Time (RNT) in minutes and is to be added to Actual Bottom Time (ABT).

Blue area indicates adjusted no-decompression limits. Actual Bottom Time (ABT) should not exceed this number.

Residual Nitrogen Time (RNT)
+ Actual Bottom Time (ABT)
= Total Bottom Time (TBT)

RETURN TO TABLE ONE

PADI — DISTRIBUTED BY INTERNATIONAL PADI, INC.

PADI STANDARD SAFE DIVING PRACTICES

When diving, you will be expected to abide by standard diving practices. These practices have been compiled to reinforce what you have learned and are intended to increase your comfort and safety in diving.

As a certified PADI diver, you should:

1. Maintain good mental and physical fitness for diving. Avoid being under the influence of alcohol or dangerous drugs when diving. Keep proficient in diving skills, striving to increase them through continuing education and reviewing them in controlled conditions after inactivity.

2. Be familiar with your dive sites. If not, obtain a formal diving orientation from a knowledgeable, local source. If diving conditions are worse than those in which you are experienced, postpone diving or select an alternate site with better conditions. Engage only in diving activities which are consistent with your training and experience.

3. Use complete, well maintained, reliable equipment with which you are familiar; and inspect it for correct fit and function prior to each dive. Deny use of your equipment to uncertified divers. Always have a buoyancy control device and submersible pressure gauge when scuba diving. Recognize the desirability of an alternate source of air and a low-pressure buoyancy-control inflation system.

4. Listen carefully to dive briefings and directions, and respect the advice of those supervising your diving activities.

5. Adhere to the buddy system throughout every dive. Plan dives, including communications, procedures for reuniting in case of separation, and emergency procedures, with your buddy.

6. Be proficient in dive table usage. Make all dives no-decompression dives and allow a margin of safety. Have a means to monitor depth and time under water. Limit maximum depth to your level of training and experience. Ascend at a rate of 60 feet per minute.

7. Maintain proper buoyancy. Adjust weighting at the surface for neutral buoyancy with no air in the buoyancy control device. Maintain neutral buoyancy while under water. Be buoyant for surface swimming and resting. Have weights clear for easy removal, and establish buoyancy when in distress while diving.

8. Breathe properly for diving. Never breath hold or skip breathe when breathing compressed air, and avoid excessive hyperventilation when breath hold diving. Avoid overexertion while in and under the water and dive within your limitations.

9. Use a boat, float, or other surface support station whenever feasible.

10. Know and obey local diving laws and regulations, including fish and game and dive flag laws.

Sample Emergency Information Card for Divers
(Can be used as original for printing.)

(Front)

DIVER EMERGENCY INFORMATION CARD

Name _____ Birth Date_____

Address_____

In emergency contact _____

Address _____ Phone ( ) _____

Medical Alert Info _____

Required Medications _____ Blood Type _____

Personal Physician_____ Phone ( ) _____

In an emergency, I hereby authorize medical treatment and/or treatment in a recompression chamber.

_____   _____
Signature   Date

_____
Signature of parent or guardian if under age 18

(Back)

INFORMATION TO BE SENT WITH VICTIM IN AN EMERGENCY:

Background of accident _____

_____

_____

_____

Symptoms observed _____

_____

_____

_____ Time _____

First Aid Given _____

_____

_____ Time _____

DIVE TRAVEL QUIZ

Q: What do these diving resorts have in common?

A: They are all part of the PADI Travel Network — the best diving has to offer.

When you're ready for fun, sun and the best in dive travel, keep it in the family...The PADI Family. Travel arrangements made through the PADI Travel Network offer PADI Divers the very best in selection and service with PADI Dive Resorts throughout the world. Everything diving is at your PADI Dive Center.

PADI TRAVEL NETWORK

Call toll free: 1-800-729-7234, Ext. 7.

FOR DIVING EMERGENCIES CALL
(919) 684-8111
24 HOURS   7 DAYS A WEEK

FOR INFORMATION CALL **(919) 684-2948**   MONDAY-FRIDAY 9-5 E.S.T.

Becoming a PADI Instructor

As a PADI Divemaster, you are likely to continue your training and become a PADI Instructor. To become a PADI Instructor you must first complete a PADI Instructor Development Course (IDC), and then pass a PADI Instructor Examination (IE). During the IE you will be given a written examination in five areas of diving theory: physics, physiology, equipment, skills and environment, and the Recreational Dive Planner (both the

Table and The Wheel). During your IDC you will receive very little formal training regarding diving theory. Therefore, the knowledge you acquire during your Divemaster training will be critical to your success on the IE exams. To help candidates prepare for the IE theory exams, the following Study Guidelines have been developed. You must become thoroughly familiar with them prior to attending your IE.

PADI Instructor Examination
Written Final Exams Study Guidelines

Use the guidelines in this document to help you prepare for the following written Final Exams administered at all PADI Instructor Examinations (IEs):

- General Skills And Environment
- Physiology
- Equipment
- Physics
- Recreational Dive Planner

1. Review academic diving information presented in the following PADI books (be sure you've mastered the academic objectives in each of the diver manuals):

   a. PADI *Open Water Diver Manual*
   b. PADI *Advanced Diver Manual*
   c. PADI *Rescue Diver Manual*
   d. PADI *Divemaster Manual*
   e. PADI *Encyclopedia of Recreational Diving*

   If these books are not available (or they do not exist in your primary language), other diving texts with detailed, elaborated academic diving information may be used.

2. Complete the PADI standard final exams for each of the following courses: Open Water Diver, Rescue Diver and Divemaster. On these exams, be able to identify the correct answer for each question. If the question is of the multiple choice type, you must also be able to explain why the other choices are incorrect.

3. Complete the PADI Instructor Preassessment Exam in the back of your *Instructor Development Course Candidate Workbook*. Your performance on this exam will be a general indicator of your knowledge of diving theory and information. Concentrate your study efforts in the areas of weakness indicated by the preassessment exam.

   NOTE: As with any preassessment document, successful mastery does not ensure success with the actual IE exams. *At the IE you are expected to have a thorough (instructor-level) knowledge of critical diving information and concepts.*

4. Questions on all PADI exams are *criterion-referenced,* meaning they relate directly to one or more performance objectives. Because these performance objectives are the basis on which PADI materials are written, the correct responses to all questions can be found within PADI materials.

   The following list of objectives were used to construct the IE written Final Exams. As a result, a thorough understanding of these objectives provide you with a solid foundation of knowledge for taking the exams. You must do more, however, than simply memorize responses to the objectives — you must be able to solve *never-before-encountered problems* and *identify specific applications* of the concepts involved. The objectives are listed according to exam topic.

5. PADI's *Diving Knowledge Workbook* is the ultimate preparation tool for the Final Exams administered at PADI IEs. The workbook is a unique way to self-study all of the objectives listed below. For each objective, the *Diving Knowledge Workbook* has several multiple-choice questions (questions much like those on the IE Final Exams). Each section has an answer key with correct answers to the questions. Accompanying each answer is rationale for how the correct answer was derived. The instructional design of the workbook helps you keep track of your progress, clearly indicating your strengths and weaknesses.

   NOTE: Although *The Encyclopedia of Recreational Diving* is a convenient assembly of academic diving knowledge, information on each objective can be obtained from other diving manuals and texts in various languages.

A. General Skills And Environment

   A PADI Instructor must be able to:

   1. State the maximum altitude above which special procedures are required for the use of most dive tables, and explain why diving at altitude requires special consideration. (*The Encyclopedia of Recreational Diving* and the PADI *Open Water*

Diver Manual)

2. Explain how tides are caused and why diving conditions are usually best at *slack tide*. (*The Encyclopedia of Recreational Diving* and the PADI *Divemaster Manual*)

3. Define the term *environmental orientation* and explain for whom such an orientation is intended. (PADI *Divemaster Manual*)

4. Explain the proper procedure for executing a Controlled Emergency Swimming Ascent. (PADI *Open Water Diver Manual*)

5. Define the term *neutral buoyancy* and describe how to execute a buoyancy check at the surface. (PADI *Open Water Diver Manual*)

6. Demonstrate the thirteen PADI Standard Hand Signals and explain the meaning of each. (PADI *Open Water Diver Manual*)

7. Explain what action should be taken with a victim of a near-drowning accident. (*The Encyclopedia of Recreational Diving* and the PADI *Rescue Diver Manual*)

8. List at least three common signs/symptoms of marine life injuries. (*The Encyclopedia of Recreational Diving* and the PADI *Rescue Diver Manual*)

9. Explain why an unconscious, non-breathing diver should be resuscitated while being towed to shore even if no pulse is suspected. (PADI *Rescue Diver Manual*)

10. Explain what action should be taken for a diver suffering from decompression sickness, and under what circumstances the victim should be taken back into the water for recompression. (*The Encyclopedia of Recreational Diving* and the PADI *Rescue Diver Manual*)

11. State the compression-to-ventilation ratio for administering one-person CPR. (PADI *Rescue Diver Manual*)

12. Given the nature of the circulation of major ocean currents (Coriolis effect), state the direction of flow for such currents in relation to the coastline of any continent. (*The Encyclopedia of Recreational Diving*)

13. State the guideline for the recovery of a negatively buoyant object without the assistance of a lift bag. (*The Encyclopedia of Recreational Diving*)

14. List the minimum suggested equipment necessary to safely engage in night diving activities. (*The Encyclopedia of Recreational Diving*)

15. State the most accurate means of measuring distance under water without the use of a calibrated measuring device. (PADI *Advanced Diver Manual*)

16. List at least two factors that dictate the type of pattern to be used when searching for an underwater object. (PADI *Advanced Diver Manual*)

17. List at least three guidelines divers should follow to help protect the marine environment. (PADI *Divemaster Manual*)

18. State the diving skill most useful in avoiding damage to the marine environment. (*The Encyclopedia of Recreational Diving*)

B. Physics

A PADI Instructor must be able to:

1. Explain why water is able to dissipate body heat faster than air, at what rate this occurs and what effect this has on the diver. (*The Encyclopedia of Recreational Diving*)

2. Explain the behavior of light as it passes from an air/water interface and what effect this has on the diver. (*The Encyclopedia of Recreational Diving*)

3. Define the *visual reversal* phenomenon and explain its effect on the diver. (*The Encyclopedia of Recreational Diving*)

4. Explain why sound travels faster in air than in water, by approximate-ly how much and what effect this has on the diver. (*The Encyclopedia of Recreational Diving*)

5. State Archimedes' Principle and calculate the buoyancy required to either lift or sink an object in both fresh- and sea-water. (*The Encyclopedia of Recreational Diving*)

6. Define the terms *absolute, ambient* and *gauge pressures* and calculate the pressure at any depth as expressed by these terms in both fresh- and seawater. (*The Encyclopedia of Recreational Diving*)

7. Explain the relationship between pressure and volume on a flexible gas-filled container, and calculate (in increments of whole atmospheres) the changes that will occur to that container as it is raised and lowered in the water column. (*The Encyclopedia of Recreational Diving*)

8. Explain the relationship between depth and the density of the air a diver breathes, and calculate this relationship in increments of whole atmospheres. (*The Encyclopedia of Recreational Diving*)

9. Given a diver's air consumption rate at one depth, calculate (in increments of whole atmospheres) how that consumption rate changes with depth. (*The Encyclopedia of Recreational Diving*)

10. Describe how the behavior of a gas within both a flexible and inflexible container is affected by changes in pressure and temperature. (*The Encyclopedia of Recreational Diving*)

11. Given their percentages, calculate the partial pressure of gases in a mixture at any depth. (*The Encyclopedia of Recreational Diving*)

12. Explain the effect of breathing contaminated air mixtures at depth, and calculate the equivalent effect such contamination would have upon the diver at the surface. (*The Encyclopedia of Recreational Diving*)

13. Explain what will occur to a gas saturated at high pressure when the pressure on gas in contact with the liquid is quickly reduced. (*The Encyclopedia of Recreational Diving*)

14. Define *supersaturation* and explain what conditions are necessary for gas bubbles to form in a supersaturated liquid. (*The Encyclopedia of Recreational Diving*)

Physiology

A PADI Instructor must be able to:

1. Name the substance within the blood that aids in the transport of oxygen. (*The Encyclopedia of Recreational Diving*)

2. Explain how proper diving techniques and equipment can help avoid exhaustion and excessive buildup of carbon dioxide. (*The Encyclopedia of Recreational Diving*)

3. Explain the physiological mechanism by which voluntary hyperventilation enables a diver to extend breath-holding time. (*The Encyclopedia of Recreational Diving*)

4. Explain the physiological mechanism that causes a *carotid sinus reflex,* and how this affects the diver. (*The Encyclopedia of Recreational Diving*)

5. Explain the physiological mechanism that causes a *shallow water blackout* and why this condition usually occurs during ascent rather than descent. (*The Encyclopedia of Recrea-*

tional Diving)

6. Explain the physiological effect of increased carbon monoxide levels (including cigarette smoking) on the diver and how it can be avoided. (*The Encyclopedia of Recreational Diving*)

7. Define the term *silent bubbles* as it relates to decompression sickness. (*The Encyclopedia of Recreational Diving*)

8. Explain why victims of decompression sickness are given pure oxygen as a first aid measure. (*The Encyclopedia of Recreational Diving*)

9. Explain the cause of nitrogen narcosis, state the approximate depth at which the disorder occurs and list three common signs/symptoms. (*The Encyclopedia of Recreational Diving*)

10. Explain the physiological mechanism of decompression sickness, and list the common susceptibility factors that can contribute to its occurrence. (*The Encyclopedia of Recreational Diving*)

11. Define the term *barotrauma,* and how it can occur to the lungs, sinuses and ears of the diver during both ascent and descent. (*The Encyclopedia of Recreational Diving*)

12. Define the term *vertigo* and explain the mechanism by which this normally occurs in the diver. (*The Encyclopedia of Recreational Diving*)

13. Describe the basic anatomy of the ear and which areas/structures are most affected by changing pressures. (*The Encyclopedia of Recreational Diving*)

14. Compare and contrast the various signs/symptoms of decompression sickness and air embolism. (*The Encyclopedia of Recreational Diving*)

15. State the most serious form of lung-expansion injury in diving and how it occurs, and what factors can contribute to its occurrence. (*The Encyclopedia of Recreational Diving*)

D. Equipment

A PADI Instructor must be able to:

1. Explain the meaning of each legally required mark that appears on the neck of a scuba tank including: alloy designation, hydrostatic test date, working pressure, and overpressurization designation. (*The Encyclopedia of Recreational Diving*)

2. Contrast the differences between steel and aluminum scuba tanks in terms of maximum pressures, thickness and capacity. (*The Encyclopedia of Recreational Diving*)

3. Explain the purpose of a J-valve and how it is designed to work. (*The Encyclopedia of Recreational Diving*)

4. Explain the safety device and design feature that prevents an overpressurized scuba tank from exploding. (*The Encyclopedia of Recreational Diving*)

5. Explain the effect of extreme heat upon the structural integrity of a scuba tank and what should be done in the event tanks are exposed to such conditions. (*The Encyclopedia of Recreational Diving*)

6. Explain how scuba tanks are hydrostatically tested and to what pressures these tests are conducted. (*The Encyclopedia of Recreational Diving*)

7. List at least three reasons a scuba tank should be visually inspected annually. (*The Encyclopedia of Recreational Diving*)

8. Explain the term *open-circuit demand* regulator and describe

what advantages this design has over other types. (*The Encyclopedia of Recreational Diving*)

9. List the major parts and explain the general function of the first and second stage of a scuba regulator. (*The Encyclopedia of Recreational Diving* and the PADI *Rescue Diver Manual.*)

10. Define the terms *balanced, unbalanced, upstream* and *downstream* as they relate to regulator design. (*The Encyclopedia of Recreational Diving*)

11. Define the term *environmental seal* and what this feature is designed to prevent. (*The Encyclopedia of Recreational Diving*)

12. Define the term *fail-safe* as it relates to regulator design and how this feature operates in the event of regulator malfunction. (*The Encyclopedia of Recreational Diving*)

13. Explain the proper procedures for the use of dive computers among buddy teams. (*The Encyclopedia of Recreational Diving*)

14. State the type of depth gauge that automatically compensates for high attitude diving. (*The Encyclopedia of Recreational Diving*)

15. List at least three equipment-related reasons why divers should always avoid maximum decompression limits.

E. Recreational Dive Planner

A PADI Instructor must be able to:

1. Explain why the RDP Surface Interval Credit Table is significantly shorter than that of the U.S. Navy tables and why such a difference is possible. (*The Encyclopedia of Recreational Diving*)

2. Explain what is meant by a *multi-tissue* decompression model and the number of tissues used in the creation of the RDP versus U.S. Navy models. (*The Encyclopedia of Recreational Diving*)

3. When diving above sea level, explain why it is critical to know the altitude at which the dive is to take place. (PADI *Advanced Diver Manual*)

4. Explain why Pressure Groups from one model/table cannot necessarily be transferred to another model/table. (*The Wheel Instructions for Use*)

5. Using both The Table and The Wheel formats of the RDP, demonstrate how to find a No-decompression Limit (NDL), and state the procedures for Emergency Decompression and Omitted Decompression. (Sections Four and Five of the PADI *Open Water Diver Manual* and *The Wheel Instructions for Use*)

6. Using both The Table and The Wheel formats of the RDP, calculate dive profiles for three or more repetitive dives, demonstrating the correct guidelines and procedures for: determining minimum surface intervals, taking safety stops, and applying the special multiple dive rule (groups W,X,Y & Z). (Sections Four and Five of the PADI *Open Water Diver Manual* and *The Wheel Instructions for Use*)

7. State the guidelines for flying after diving and demonstrate the application of the rule for each circumstance addressed. (PADI *Open Water Diver Manual*)

8. Using The Wheel format of the RDP, demonstrate how to calculate a multilevel dive. (*The Wheel Instructions for Use*)

Index